PROGRAMMING FOR BEGINNERS

3 Books in 1
HTML + CSS + JavaScript
(Basic Fundamental Guide for Beginners)

© Copyright 2018 by _____MG Martin____ - All rights reserved.

The following Book is reproduced below with the goal of providing information that is as accurate and reliable as possible. Regardless, purchasing this Book can be seen as consent to the fact that both the publisher and the author of this book are in no way experts on the topics discussed within and that any recommendations or suggestions that are made herein are for entertainment purposes only. Professionals should be consulted as needed prior to undertaking any of the actions endorsed herein.

This declaration is deemed fair and valid by both the American Bar Association and the Committee of Publishers Association and is legally binding throughout the United States.

Furthermore, the transmission, duplication, or reproduction of any of the following work including specific information will be considered an illegal act irrespective of whether it is done electronically or in print. This extends to creating a secondary or tertiary copy of the work or a recorded copy and is only allowed with the express written consent from the Publisher. All additional rights reserved.

The information in the following pages is broadly considered to be a truthful and accurate account of facts, and as such any inattention, use or misuse of the information in question by the reader will render any resulting actions solely under their purview. There are no scenarios in which the publisher or the original author of this work can be, in any fashion, deemed liable for any hardship or damages that may befall them after undertaking information described herein.

Additionally, the information in the following pages is intended only for informational purposes and should thus be thought of as universal. As befitting its nature, it is presented without assurance regarding its prolonged validity or interim quality. Trademarks are mentioned without written consent and can in no way be considered an endorsement from the trademark holder.

TABLE OF CONTENTS

HTML

Basic Fundamental Guide for Beginners

Introduction 3

Chapter 1 : Getting Started With Basic HTML Tags 4

What are elements, tags, and attributes? 4

How do I get started with my first web page? 6

How can I change the appearance of the
elements on my web page? 10

Chapter 2 : Creating HTML Lists And Tables 31

How can I display my content as a list? 31

How can I display my content as a table? 40

What other ways can I display my content? 48

Chapter 3 : Creating HTML Forms And Handling Input 50

What kinds of input can I accept from users? 50

How can I customize the forms on my web page? 57

Chapter 4 : HTML And CSS 64

What is CSS? 64

How can CSS enhance my web page? 66

Chapter 5 : Using Div Elements 73

Conclusion 76

CSS

Basic Fundamental Guide for Beginners

Introduction 79

Chapter 1 : Taking Off With CSS 80
    How do CSS and HTML work together? 80
    How can I use CSS with my HTML? 82
    How should I format my CSS? 87

Chapter 2 : Using CSS Selectors 90
    Simple Selectors 90
    Attribute Selectors 95
    Multiple Selectors 97

Chapter 3 : CSS Layout Basics 99

Chapter 4 : Polishing Your Web Pages With CSS 121

Chapter 5 : CSS Animations 125

Chapter 6 : Trends in CSS - Fixed Width Sites 128

Chapter 7 : Trends In CSS - Responsive Design 132

Conclusion 138

JavaScript

Basic Fundamental Guide for Beginners

Introduction 141

Chapter 1 : History of JavaScript 142

Chapter 2 : How JavaScript is Used 149

Chapter 3 : How to Program in JavaScript 151

    Setting Up 151

    Data and Variables 153

    Math in JavaScript 158

    Foundations of Logic 160

    Control Flow 101: Conditional Statements 164

    Arrays 166

    Control Flow 102: Loops 170

    Functions 175

    Object-Oriented Programming: An Introduction 177

Chapter 4 : The Future of JavaScript 180

Conclusion 182

HTML

Basic Fundamental Guide for Beginners

Introduction

Congratulations and thank you for purchasing *HTML: Basic Fundamental Guide For Beginners*! Whether you're interested in learning HTML to build your own basic website or you'd just like to expand your understanding of markup languages, this book is a great starting point and will provide you with easy-to-understand explanations and examples. In no time you'll be able to use your newly learned HTML skills to create a simple yet functional website.

Never used a programming or markup language before? Don't panic! You don't need much to begin—in fact, all you need to get started with learning HTML is a simple program for editing text (like Notepad or TextEdit) and a web browser to view your creations. In the following chapters, you'll learn not only what HTML is and what it can be used for but also gain an understanding of basic HTML through descriptions and samples that you can easily reproduce yourself. Excited about designing your very own website? By the time you complete this book, you will be able to apply what you've learned to create a simple page with different fonts, eye-catching colors, a unique layout, tables, lists, and even a form that will accept input from a user!

There are many books available on this subject, so thanks again for choosing this one. Good luck and have fun getting started with HTML!

Chapter 1

Getting Started With Basic HTML Tags

Before getting started with writing your first small chunk of HTML, it's necessary that you understand what HTML is. Literally, HTML is an initialism for HyperText Markup Language, which is a set of codes and symbols used to mark up a file so that a web browser knows how to display the content of the file. *Without* HTML, a browser would just display your web page as plain text without any sorts of fonts, colors, or layout; *with* HTML, a browser knows how to display your web page in exactly the style and format that you want. Generally speaking, HTML defines the way that a web page—and the internet as a whole—will appear to users.

In order to give a browser instructions about how to display a file, HTML uses something called tags to signify the beginnings and ends of elements. These tags contain information called attributes which allow a browser to know how the element should appear. The next few sections discuss how elements, tags, and attributes work to define how your web page content will look.

What are elements, tags, and attributes?

In HTML, an element is a single component of your web page. Generally, each element on your page will have both a start and end tag as well as some sort of content, though certain "empty elements" only require a start tag. Both kinds of tags are labels enclosed in the <> symbols that a browser uses to know how to display a page, but the tags themselves are not displayed. Tags are commonly written in lowercase despite the fact that HTML is not case sensitive. Take a look at the format of an HTML element:

<sometagname> A little bit of content </sometagname>

You can see that the element begins with a tag called "sometagname" which is enclosed in the <> symbols. At the end of the content, you can see the end tag. You'll notice that the end tag is almost identical to the start tag with the addition of the / symbol before the tag name inside the <> symbols. Some elements will display accurately even if the end tag is missing, but sometimes a missing end tag will create an error, so it's best to ensure that your end tags are always in place.

The start tag for an element can define attributes for the element which can give the browser a little bit more information about how the element should be displayed. For instance, an attribute of a link element could be the URL destination for the link. Attributes of an image might include its display height and width. For text, attributes could be styling information like what color, size, or font it should be displayed as. An element can have multiple attributes, so you can fully customize the components of your web pages.

Attributes are contained within the start tag after the tag name and consist of the attribute name followed by the = symbol and then the attribute information in quotation marks. The basic format should look like this:

<sometagname someattributename="attribute value">

A little bit of content

</sometagname>

Similar to the tag name, the attribute name should be written in lowercase. The attribute value should be contained in either single or double quotations. It is worth noting here that if your attribute value itself contains single or double quotation marks, you will need to use the opposite to enclose the attribute value. For instance, if your attribute value is the phrase "You're awesome!" you'll need to enclose it with double quotes, like so:

someattributename="You're awesome!"

Alternatively, if your attribute value is something like "Amanda "Mandy" Jones," then you should enclose it with single quotes:

someattributename='Amanda "Mandy" Jones'

If this seems a little overwhelming, don't worry! Over the course of the next couple of sections, you'll have the opportunity to view some actual examples of working HTML and you'll have the opportunity to gain some hands-on experience.

How do I get started with my first web page?

Now that you have a basic idea of how HTML uses tags to tell a browser how to display content, it's time to put that knowledge to use! Throughout this next section, you'll learn some ways that you can use HTML to put together a very basic web page. Open up Notepad, TextEdit, or your favorite text editor and follow along.

Note: if you're a Mac user using TextEdit, you may need to adjust some settings in order to view and save things properly. Under Preferences and then Format, you'll want to select "Plain Text," and under Open and Save, you'll need to check a box that says "Display HTML files as HTML code instead of formatted text."

The very first thing you'll need to include whenever you start writing an HTML document is the following line:

    <!DOCTYPE html>

This line is not an element even though it uses the <> symbols just like element tags do. This line is a declaration, and it lets the browser know that the document is written using HTML. If this line is not present, the browser may attempt to display the web page using some default styles, but certain elements may not show up correctly. It's important to always include this line.

The next component of your HTML file will be the root element of your page, and it will surround the remainder of the HTML in your file. This root element will have <html> start and end tags, so your HTML document so far will look like this:

    <!DOCTYPE html>
    <html>

    </html>

You'll notice that there's some space between the <html> start and end tags—that's where the rest of your elements will be written. HTML allows elements to be nested, which means an element can actually contain another element or even multiple elements. The first element that will be contained inside of the <html> root element will be the <head> element, which contains metadata or data about the HTML document. This metadata can define information like the title of a document, scripts, links to CSS stylesheets, descriptions of your web page, and styles. For this first example, we'll just be putting the title of the document you're wanting to create into the <head> element, so the HTML document will look similar to this:

    <!DOCTYPE html>

```
<html>
<head>
<title> Just an Example Web Page </title>
</head>
</html>
```

The text that is contained inside of the <title> element—in this example, Just an Example Web Page—is what will show up in a browser tab as the name of the page. It's also what the page will be called if you add it to your favorites or find it somewhere online, such as in results from a search engine.

You may notice that in our sample, the <head> element start and end tags are indented under the root <html> element, and after that the <title> element is indented within the <head> element. This is not necessary, but it can help when writing your HTML document to see how elements are laid out. The page will display the same whether or not the element tags are indented, however, so it's up to you to write your HTML documents in whichever way you feel the most comfortable.

Of course, you won't just want your web page to be a blank page with a title, so you'll need to have a space to put all of the content you want to be displayed on your page. You'll do this within another element within the <html> element called the <body> element. It will come after the <head> element like so:

```
<!DOCTYPE html>
<html>
<head>
<title> Just an Example Webpage </title>
</head>
<body>

</body>
</html>
```

The <body> element of your HTML document will contain everything that is visible on your web page like text, pictures, links, and media. For this simple example, we'll just be adding a couple lines of text to your page: one large heading and one smaller paragraph. Now, your HTML document will look like this:

```
<!DOCTYPE html>
<html>
<head>
<title> Just an Example Webpage </title>
</head>
<body>
    <h1> Example of headings in HTML. </h1>
    <p> Example of paragraphs in HTML. </p>
    <p> Second example of paragraphs in HTML </p>
</body>
</html>
```

The heading element starts with the <h1> tag and ends with the </h1> tag, and the paragraph elements start and end with the <p> and </p> tags. You can see that the heading and the paragraph elements are separate from each other but are all contained within the <body> element. Make sure to use end tags, and be sure to put them in the appropriate places.

That's it! You now have a simple HTML document that will display a simple web page in a browser. In order to test it out, you'll first need to save your HTML document with the correct file extension. Click "Save as" in the menu, and then put the file name **myexamplewebpage.html** in the "File name" box. Don't forget the .html extension! Next, change the "Save as type" to "All Files (*.*)" and click Save. Now you can open your HTML file in your browser window either by double-clicking on it from where you saved it or by clicking the file with your right mouse button and picking "Open with." When your page opens, it should look something like this:

This line is a heading.

This line is a paragraph.

This line is also a paragraph.

In the URL bar, you should be able to see the file path to the HTML document you created; it will probably look similar to this, but not exactly the same. You can see from this example how the page title, heading, and paragraphs are displayed. The browser utilizes the HTML tags to decide how to show the text content, but the tags themselves are not shown.

How can I change the appearance of the elements on my web page?

Now that you have a basic framework for your HTML pages, you'll undoubtedly want to start adding custom elements to create a page that fits your personal needs. Check out some of the different tags below that you can use to completely customize your sites:

<title> </title>

The <title> element contains the name of your web page, which is displayed in a browser tab or within search engine results. Be sure to title your page something informative!

\<style> \</style>

These tags contain information about the default styles your document will use and are located inside the \<head> element of your HTML document. Alternatively, one can set the style for an individual element within its start tag.

\<meta>

This tag and its attributes define information about your web page, like a page description, page author, or keywords relevant to your page. This tag is contained in the \<head> element and does not show anything on your page itself.

\<script> \</script>

These tags contain JavaScript code that can be used elsewhere on your page to perform actions like manipulating images or validating forms.

\<p> \</p>

These tags signify the beginning and end of a paragraph. You used these in the example in the previous section. A paragraph is simply text that is spaced apart from surrounding elements.

\<b> \</b>

These tags signify that the contained text should be bold.

\<u> \</u>

These tags signify that the contained text should be underlined.

\<i> \</i>

These tags signify that the contained text should be italicized.

<del> </del>

These tags signify that the contained text was deleted and the text is displayed with a line through it.

<mark> </mark>

These tags signify that the contained text should be highlighted.

<h1> </h1>

These tags are used to display a large or very important heading.

<h2> </h2>

These tags are used to display a heading that is large and important, but less so than h1.

<h3> </h3>

These tags are used to display smaller or less important heading than h2.

<h4> </h4>

These tags are used to display smaller or less important heading than h3.

<h5> </h5>

These tags are used to display smaller or less important heading than h4.

<h6> </h6>

These tags are used to display the smallest-sized or least important heading.

<a> </a>

These tags are used to define a link. You'll use the href attribute to specify the destination for the link and the link will be displayed as the text that is placed between the two given tags.

<img>

This tag is used to define an image and does not use an end tag. You can use attributes to control the source file for the image, the image size, and any alternative text for the image.

<button> </button>

These tags signify a button that can be clicked. You can use buttons along with JavaScript to perform certain actions when the buttons are clicked.

**
**

This tag signifies a line break and doesn't require an end tag. A line break is simply an empty line. You can use one or multiple line breaks between the elements on your page to space them out and prevent your layout from appearing jumbled.

HTML also uses certain element tags to help define the layout of your web page, such as the following:

<header> </header>

This element defines a section or document header.

<nav> </nav>

This element contains the navigation links for a web page.

<section> </section>

This element determines a section within a document.

<aside> </aside>

This element contains additional sidebar content on a web page.

<footer> </footer>

This element defines a section or document footer.

<details> </details>

This element contains additional details about the page.

You'll also want to familiarize yourself with the attributes that can be used with each of these tags. Some of the most common and important ones are as follows:

href

This attribute defines the URL for a link element. You'll want to use the full URL, including the http:// at the beginning.

src

This attribute signifies where the source file for an image can be found. This can be a file path or a URL. If the file in question and the HTML document are both saved in the same folder, you can simply use the filename and extension here; otherwise, you should use an absolute file path.

title

This attribute gives additional information about an element which is displayed when a cursor hovers over it. This can help users understand how to use certain aspects of your web page.

alt

This attribute provides alt text for an image which is displayed when the image itself can't be shown.

id

This attribute assigns a unique id to an element. Each id should only be used once per web page; an id is often used as a unique identifier for a particular element.

disabled

This attribute signifies that an element should be displayed as disabled on your web page. Disabled elements are usually greyed out, which prevents users from interacting with them.

height

This attribute defines how tall an element should be on your web page. It can be a set amount of pixels or even a percentage value.

width

This attribute defines how wide an element should be on your web page. It can be a set amount of pixels or even a percentage value.

style

This attribute can be used to define how an element is styled in terms of size, color, or font.

There are many other tags and attributes available for you to use, but they won't all be necessary for every web page you build, and certain elements can tend to be complex to use. For this beginner's tutorial, we'll be sticking to some of the simpler elements to create your page. Open up your text editor again and follow along!

For this example, we'll start off in the same way that we did with the first example, by beginning the document with the HTML declaration and the <html> start tag:

    <!DOCTYPE html>
    <html>

Then, we'll add some information into the <head> element, so put the <head> start tag on the next line:

    <!DOCTYPE html>
    <html>
      <head>

On the next line, we'll define the title of our web page, just like we did in our first sample:

    <!DOCTYPE html>
    <html>
      <head>
      <title> Another web page! </title>

Now we can add in something different. By using the <style> element, we can set default style information for our web page. Let's make it so that our web page has a blue background, white headings, and red paragraphs with a white background:

```
<!DOCTYPE html>
<html>
  <head>
    <title> Another web page! </title>

    <style>
        body {background-color: blue;}
        h1 {color: white;}
        p {color: red; background-color: white;}
    </style>
```

Next, let's use the <meta> element to add some information about our web page to our document, like an author, a description, and some keywords for search engines to use:

```
<!DOCTYPE html>
<html>
  <head>
        <title> Another web page! </title>
        <style>
            body {background-color: blue;}
            h1 {color: white;}
            p {color: red; background-color: white;}
        </style>
        <meta name="author" content="Your Name">
        <meta name="description" content ="A basic web page sample">
        <meta name="keywords" content="HTML, sample, beginner">
```

17

Great! If you want to define any JavaScript functions or link to a CSS stylesheet you would also do that here in the <head> element, but for now, let's end the <head> element and put some customized elements into the <body> element:

```
<!DOCTYPE html>
<html>
   <head>
      <title> Another web page! </title>
      <style>
         body {background-color: blue;}
         h1 {color: white;}
         p {color: red; background-color: white;}
      </style>
      <meta name="author" content="Your Name">
      <meta name="description" content ="A basic web page sample">
      <meta name="keywords" content="HTML, sample, beginner">
   </head>
   <body>
```

First, let's add in a few different headings. Remember in the <head> element that you set the default color for <h1> elements to white. Let's add an <h1> element without any attributes, an <h1> element with a specified color attribute, and some other heading elements with various attributes to see how their sizes and styles compare:

```
<!DOCTYPE html>
<html>
  <head>
    <title> Another web page! </title>
    <style>
        body {background-color: blue;}
        h1 {color: white;}
        p {color: red; background-color: white;}
    </style>
    <meta name="author" content="Your Name">
    <meta name="description" content ="A basic web page sample">
    <meta name="keywords" content="HTML, sample, beginner">
  </head>
  <body>
      <h1> This is a heading using the defined default style. </h1>
      <h1 style="color:aqua;"> Example of headings being given defined color attributes. </h1>
      <h2 style="text-align:center;"> Example of centering subheadings using CSS properties. </h2>
      <h3 > This is a smaller subheading with the default style. </h3>
      <h4 style="background-color:black; color:white;"> This is an even smaller subheading with a defined color and background color. </h4>
      <h5 style="text-align:right;"> This is an even smaller subheading, and it's right justified! </h5>
      <h6 style="background-color:green;"> This is the smallest heading with a defined background color. </h6>
```

Now, let's add some text and some line breaks below your headings. Remember, one is able to nest elements within other ones!

```html
<!DOCTYPE html>
<html>
    <head>
        <title> Another web page! </title>
        <style>
            body {background-color: blue;}
            h1 {color: white;}
            p {color: red; background-color: white;}
        </style>
        <meta name="author" content="Your Name">
        <meta name="description" content ="A basic web page sample">
        <meta name="keywords" content="HTML, sample, beginner">
    </head>
    <body>
        <h1> This is a heading using the defined default style. </h1>
        <h1 style="color:aqua;"> Example of headings being given defined color attributes </h1>
        <h2 style="text-align:center;"> Example of centering subheadings using CSS properties. </h2>
        <h3 > This is a smaller subheading with the default style. </h3>
        <h4 style="background-color:black; color:white;"> This is an even smaller subheading with a defined color and background color. </h4>
        <h5 style="text-align:right;"> This is an even smaller subheading, and it's right justified! </h5>
        <h6 style="background-color:green;"> This is the smallest heading with a defined background color. </h6>
```

<p> Example of paragraphs using default style definition. </p>

<p style="background-color:blue; color:black;"> Example of the background color removed and a text color defined. </p>

<p style="font-size:200%;"> Example of doubling font size in paragraph. </p>

<p style="color:black;"> Example of <b> bold </b> , <i> italicized </i> , <u> underlined </u> , and <mark> highlighted </mark> words. </p>

<p> This is an example of <br> breaking up lines in HTML. </p>

<p style="font-family:courier; background-color:black; color:white;"> Example of a different font and a defined background color and text color. </p>

<p title="Hello!"> This paragraph shows some text when you hover over it. </p>

Next, let's put a link on our page that sends the user to the Google homepage when they click it:

```
<!DOCTYPE html>
<html>
    <head>
        <title> Another web page! </title>
        <style>
            body {background-color: blue;}
            h1 {color: white;}
            p {color: red; background-color: white;}
        </style>
        <meta name="author" content="Your Name">
        <meta name="description" content ="A basic web page sample">
        <meta name="keywords" content="HTML, sample, beginner">
    </head>
    <body>
        <h1> This is a heading using the defined default style. </h1>
        <h1 style="color:aqua;"> Example of headings being given defined color attributes </h1>
        <h2 style="text-align:center;"> Example of centering subheadings using CSS properties. </h2>
        <h3 > This is a smaller subheading with the default style. </h3>
        <h4 style="background-color:black; color:white;"> This is an even smaller subheading with a defined color and background color. </h4>
        <h5 style="text-align:right;"> This is an even smaller subheading, and it's right justified! </h5>
        <h6 style="background-color:green;"> This is the smallest heading with a defined background color. </h6>

        <p> Example of paragraphs using default style definition. </p>
```

```
<p style="background-color:blue; color:black;"> Example
of the background color removed and a text color defined.
</p>
<p style="font-size:200%;"> Example of doubling font size
in paragraph. </p>
<p style="color:black;"> Example of <b> bold </b> , <i>
italicized </i> , <u> underlined </u> , and <mark>
highlighted </mark> words. </p>
<p> This is an example of <br> breaking up lines in HTML.
</p>
<p style="font-family:courier; background-color:black;
color:white;"> Example of a different font and a defined
background color and text color. </p>
<p title="Hello!"> This paragraph shows some text when
you hover over it. </p>

<a style="color:white;" href="http://www.google.com">
Outgoing anchor to Google </a>
```

Finally, let's put a picture onto your web page. You can use an image that you have saved on your computer or you can use one online. To use an image from your own computer, you'll need to save the image in the same location as your HTML document. For instance, if your HTML document is saved on your desktop, your image should also be saved on your desktop; if your HTML document is saved in a folder, your image should be saved in the same folder. Let's add an image that's saved as shapes.png:

```html
<!DOCTYPE html>
<html>
    <head>
        <title> Another web page! </title>
        <style>
            body {background-color: blue;}
            h1 {color: white;}
            p {color: red; background-color: white;}
        </style>
        <meta name="author" content="Your Name">
        <meta name="description" content ="A basic web page sample">
        <meta name="keywords" content="HTML, sample, beginner">
    </head>
    <body>
        <h1> This is a heading using the defined default style. </h1>
        <h1 style="color:aqua;"> Example of headings being given defined color attributes </h1>
        <h2 style="text-align:center;"> Example of centering subheadings using CSS properties. </h2>
        <h3 > This is a smaller subheading with the default style. </h3>
        <h4 style="background-color:black; color:white;"> This is an even smaller subheading with a defined color and background color. </h4>
        <h5 style="text-align:right;"> This is an even smaller subheading, and it's right justified! </h5>
        <h6 style="background-color:green;"> This is the smallest heading with a defined background color. </h6>
        <p> Example of paragraphs using default style definition. </p>
        <p style="background-color:blue; color:black;"> Example of the background color removed and a text color defined. </p>
```

<p style="font-size:200%;"> Example of doubling font size in paragraph. </p>

<p style="color:black;"> Example of <b> bold </b> , <i> italicized </i> , <u> underlined </u> , and <mark> highlighted </mark> words. </p>

<p> This is an example of <br> breaking up lines in HTML. </p>

<p style="font-family:courier; background-color:black; color:white;"> Example of a different font and a defined background color and text color. </p>

<p title="Hello!"> This paragraph shows some text when you hover over it. </p>

<a style="color:white;" href="http://www.google.com"> Outgoing anchor to Google </a>

<img src="shapes.png">

If you'd like to change the size of the image, you can do so using the width and height attributes. You can also add some alternative text to the image using the alt attribute:

```html
<!DOCTYPE html>
<html>
    <head>
        <title> Another web page! </title>
        <style>
            body {background-color: blue;}
            h1 {color: white;}
            p {color: red; background-color: white;}
        </style>
        <meta name="author" content="Your Name">
        <meta name="description" content ="A basic web page sample">
        <meta name="keywords" content="HTML, sample, beginner">
    </head>
    <body>
        <h1> This is a heading using the defined default style. </h1>
        <h1 style="color:aqua;"> Example of headings being given defined color attributes </h1>
        <h2 style="text-align:center;"> Example of centering subheadings using CSS properties. </h2>
        <h3 > This is a smaller subheading with the default style. </h3>
        <h4 style="background-color:black; color:white;"> This is an even smaller subheading with a defined color and background color. </h4>
        <h5 style="text-align:right;"> This is an even smaller subheading, and it's right justified! </h5>
        <h6 style="background-color:green;"> This is the smallest heading with a defined background color. </h6>
        <p> Example of paragraphs using default style definition. </p>
        <p style="background-color:blue; color:black;"> Example of the background color removed and a text color defined. </p>
```

<p style="font-size:200%;"> Example of doubling font size in paragraph. </p>

<p style="color:black;"> Example of <b> bold </b> , <i> italicized </i> , <u> underlined </u> , and <mark> highlighted </mark> words. </p>

<p> This is an example of <br> breaking up lines in HTML. </p>

<p style="font-family:courier; background-color:black; color:white;"> Example of a different font and a defined background color and text color. </p>

<p title="Hello!"> This paragraph shows some text when you hover over it. </p>

<a style="color:white;" href="http://www.google.com"> Outgoing anchor to Google </a>

<img src="shapes.png">

<img src="shapes.png" width="750" height="500" alt="A square, a circle, and a triangle.">

Great! Now, close the <body> and <html> elements, and you should have an HTML document that looks like this:

```html
<!DOCTYPE html>
<html>
    <head>
        <title> Another web page! </title>
        <style>
            body {background-color: blue;}
            h1 {color: white;}
            p {color: red; background-color: white;}
        </style>
        <meta name="author" content="Your Name">
        <meta name="description" content ="A basic web page sample">
        <meta name="keywords" content="HTML, sample, beginner">
    </head>
    <body>
        <h1> This is a heading using the defined default style. </h1>
        <h1 style="color:aqua;"> Example of headings being given defined color attributes </h1>
        <h2 style="text-align:center;"> Example of centering subheadings using CSS properties. </h2>
        <h3 > This is a smaller subheading with the default style. </h3>
        <h4 style="background-color:black; color:white;"> This is an even smaller subheading with a defined color and background color. </h4>
        <h5 style="text-align:right;"> This is an even smaller subheading, and it's right justified! </h5>
        <h6 style="background-color:green;"> This is the smallest heading with a defined background color. </h6>
        <p> Example of paragraphs using default style definition. </p>
        <p style="background-color:blue; color:black;"> Example of the background color removed and a text color defined. </p>
```

```
<p style="font-size:200%;"> Example of doubling font size in paragraph. </p>
<p style="color:black;"> Example of <b> bold </b> , <i> italicized </i> , <u> underlined </u> , and <mark> highlighted </mark> words. </p>
<p> This is an example of <br> breaking up lines in HTML. </p>
<p style="font-family:courier; background-color:black; color:white;"> Example of a different font and a defined background color and text color. </p>
<p title="Hello!"> This paragraph shows some text when you hover over it. </p>
<a style="color:white;" href="http://www.google.com"> Outgoing anchor to Google </a>
<br>
<br>
<img src="shapes.png">
<br>
<br>
<img src="shapes.png" width="750" height="500" alt="A square, a circle, and a triangle.">
    </body>
</html>
```

When you save this document with a .html extension and open it using a browser, it will look something like this:

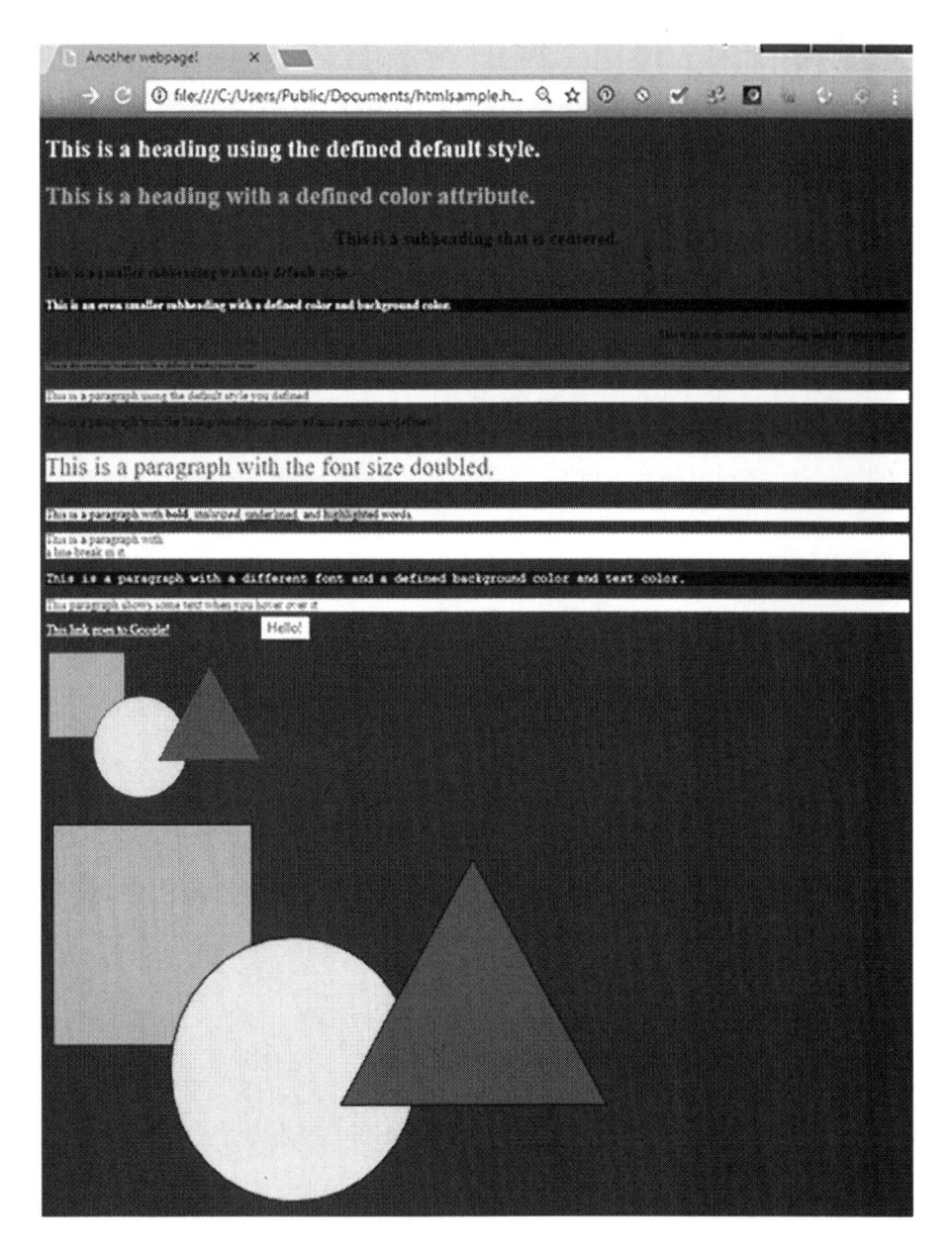

Congratulations! You've made an HTML page with customized elements. Feel free to play around with the tags and attributes for these sample elements to make a simple web page that suits your personal needs. Try to practice creating different custom elements, like an image that links to another website, or a heading that shows a message when you hover over it with a cursor.

Chapter 2

Creating HTML Lists And Tables

In addition to headings and paragraphs, you may want to display your text in other formats, such as a list or a table. Fortunately, HTML makes this simple to do using tags just like the ones you practiced using in the previous chapter. Follow along through the next sections to see additional ways you can format the content of your web page.

How can I display my content as a list?

If you'd like to display a portion of the content on your web page as a list, you actually have a couple of different options to do so. For lists in which you would like the items to have a defined order, you can create what is called an ordered list, which uses numbers, letters, or numerals next to the list items. Ordered lists are defined using the <ol> tag, and each item in the list uses a <li> tag. For instance, if you'd like to create a list of race participants by the order in which they finished, you might have something like this:

```
<ol>
    <li> Susan </li>
    <li> Mark </li>
    <li> Amanda </li>
    <li> Jon </li>
</ol>
```

which will number the participants from 1 to 4. You can use the **type** attribute to change the numbering system to upper or lowercase letters or upper or lowercase Roman numerals like so:

```
<ol type="1">
   <li> Susan </li>
   <li> Mark </li>
   <li> Amanda </li>
   <li> Jon </li>
</ol>
<ol type="A">
   <li> Susan </li>
   <li> Mark </li>
   <li> Amanda </li>
   <li> Jon </li>
</ol>
<ol type="a">
   <li> Susan </li>
   <li> Mark </li>
   <li> Amanda </li>
   <li> Jon </li>
</ol>
<ol type="I">
   <li> Susan </li>
   <li> Mark </li>
   <li> Amanda </li>
   <li> Jon </li>
</ol>
<ol type="i">
   <li> Susan </li>
   <li> Mark </li>
   <li> Amanda </li>
   <li> Jon </li>
</ol>
```

If you'd like, you also have the option to start numbering your ordered list from a specified point using the **start** attribute:

```
<ol start="10">
   <li> Brian </li>
   <li> David </li>
   <li> Lynn </li>
   <li> Sabrina </li>
</ol>
<ol start="50">
   <li> Louise </li>
   <li> Morgan </li>
   <li> Jana </li>
   <li> Peter </li>
</ol>
```

Alternatively, if the order of your list items doesn't matter, you can create an unordered list. Unordered lists use markers or bullets to mark individual list items, and are defined using the <ul> tag. Similarly to ordered lists, each individual list item is defined with the <li> tag, as follows:

```
<ul>
   <li> square </li>
   <li> triange </li>
   <li> rectangle </li>
   <li> circle </li>
</ul>
```

Unordered lists can also be customized using the **style** attribute. The default style is to use bullets, but you can also use squares, circles, or no markers at all to mark each item in your list, like so:

```
<ul style="list-style-type:square">
   <li> square </li>
   <li> triange </li>
```

```
    <li> rectangle </li>
    <li> circle </li>
</ul>
<ul style="list-style-type:circle">
    <li> square </li>
    <li> triange </li>
    <li> rectangle </li>
    <li> circle </li>
</ul>
<ul style="list-style-type:none">
    <li> square </li>
    <li> triange </li>
    <li> rectangle </li>
    <li> circle </li>
</ul>
```

You can further customize your lists by using the <b> , <i> , <u> , <a>, or <mark> tags around your text, just like you did with your paragraph text in the previous chapter. You can also nest lists within lists, like so:

```
<ul>
    <li> words </li>
        <ul>
            <li> normal </li>
            <li> <b> bold </b> </li>
            <li> <i> italicized </i> </li>
            <li> <mark> highlighted </mark> </li>
            <li> <a href="http://www.google.com"> link </a> </li>
        </ul>

    <li> numbers </li>
        <ol>
            <li> one </li>
            <li> two </li>
```

```
            <li> three </li>
        </ol>
</ul>
```

Let's create another simple web page using headings and lists to see how different list types and styles appear in a browser. Type or copy and paste this next bit of HTML into your text editor:

```
<!DOCTYPE html>
<html>
   <head>
            <title> Lists! </title>
   </head>
   <body>
            <h3> An ordered list: </h3>
            <ol>
                    <li> Susan </li>
                    <li> Mark </li>
                    <li> Amanda </li>
                    <li> Jon </li>
            </ol>

            <h3> An ordered list using uppercase letters: </h3>
            <ol type="A">
                    <li> Susan </li>
                    <li> Mark </li>
                    <li> Amanda </li>
                    <li> Jon </li>
            </ol>


            <h3> An ordered list using lowercase letters: </h3>
            <ol type="a">
                    <li> Susan </li>
                    <li> Mark </li>
```

```
        <li> Amanda </li>
        <li> Jon </li>
</ol>


    <h3> An ordered list using uppercase roman numerals: </h3>
<ol type="I">
        <li> Susan </li>
        <li> Mark </li>
        <li> Amanda </li>
        <li> Jon </li>
</ol>


    <h3> An ordered list using lowercase roman numerals: </h3>
<ol type="i">
        <li> Susan </li>
        <li> Mark </li>
        <li> Amanda </li>
        <li> Jon </li>
</ol>


<h3> An ordered list starting at 10: </h3>
<ol start="10">
        <li> Brian </li>
        <li> David </li>
        <li> Lynn </li>
        <li> Sabrina </li>
</ol>


<h3> An unordered list: </h3>
<ul>
        <li> square </li>
        <li> triange </li>
```

```html
        <li> rectangle </li>
        <li> circle </li>
</ul>

<h3> An unordered list using square markers: </h3>
<ul style="list-style-type:square">
        <li> square </li>
        <li> triange </li>
        <li> rectangle </li>
        <li> circle </li>
</ul>

<h3> An unordered list using circle markers: </h3>
<ul style="list-style-type:circle">
        <li> square </li>
        <li> triange </li>
        <li> rectangle </li>
        <li> circle </li>
</ul>

<h3> An unordered list using no markers: </h3>
<ul style="list-style-type:none">
        <li> square </li>
        <li> triange </li>
        <li> rectangle </li>
        <li> circle </li>
</ul>


<h3> Nested lists: </h3>
<ul>
        <li> words </li>
                <ul>
                        <li> normal </li>
                        <li> <b> bold </b> </li>
```

```
                    <li> <i> italicized </i> </li>
                    <li> <mark> highlighted </mark> </li>
                    <li> <a href="http://www.google.com"> link </a> </li>
                </ul>
                <li> numbers </li>
                <ol>
                    <li> one </li>
                    <li> two </li>
                    <li> three </li>
                </ol>
            </ul>
        </body>
</html>
```

Now save the document with a .html extension and then open it up using a browser. Your web page should look something like this:

An ordered list:

1. Susan
2. Mark
3. Amanda
4. Jon

An ordered list using uppercase letters:

A. Susan
B. Mark
C. Amanda
D. Jon

An ordered list using lowercase letters:

a. Susan
b. Mark
c. Amanda
d. Jon

An ordered list using uppercase roman numerals:

I. Susan
II. Mark
III. Amanda
IV. Jon

An ordered list using lowercase roman numerals:

i. Susan
ii. Mark
iii. Amanda
iv. Jon

An ordered list starting at 10:

10. Brian
11. David
12. Lynn
13. Sabrina

An unordered list:

- square
- triange
- rectangle
- circle

An unordered list using square markers:

- square
- triange
- rectangle
- circle

An unordered list using circle markers:

- square
- triange
- rectangle
- circle

An unordered list using no markers:

square
triange
rectangle
circle

Nested lists:

- words
    - normal
    - **bold**
    - *italicized*
    - highlighted
    - link
- numbers
    1. one
    2. two
    3. three

How can I display my content as a table?

You may also occasionally want to display content as a table on your web page. You can accomplish this by using the <table> , <tr> , <th> and <td> tags. The <tr> tag signifies a row of the table, while the <th> and <td> tags specify table headers and table date respectively. Consider

40

a table with three columns that contain the first name, last name, and birthday for a set of individuals. Your HTML might look something like this:

```
<table>
    <tr>
        <th> First Name </th>
        <th> Last Name </th>
        <th> Birthday </th>
    </tr>
    <tr>
        <td> Rebecca </td>
        <td> Jones </td>
        <td> May 2 </td>
    </tr>
    <tr>
        <td> Tony </td>
        <td> White </td>
        <td> April 14 </td>
    </tr>
    <tr>
        <td> Jamie </td>
        <td> Parker </td>
        <td> August 27 </td>
    </tr>
</table>
```

You can use attributes to customize the size and text alignment of the elements in your table. For instance, you can alter the <table> element's **style** attribute to set your table to cover a set width or the whole width of your web page, and you can use the **text-align** attributes for the headers and cells to left align, center align, or right align your text. *Note: you can put the text-align attribute into the start tags of each of your cells, but if you're using the same formatting for an entire table, it will* *probably be easier to include this styling information within the document's **<head>** element, like you did in Chapter 1.*

Give it a try! Type the following HTML into your text editor:

```
<!DOCTYPE html>
<html>
    <head>
        <title> Tables! </title>
        <style>
            th {text-align:left;}
            td {text-align:center;}
        </style>
    </head>
    <body>
        <h3> A table with 3 columns that spans 75% of the window width: </h3>
        <table style="width:75%">
            <tr style="background-color:grey;">
                <th> First Name </th>
                <th> Last Name </th>
                <th> Birthday </th>
            </tr>
            <tr style="color:green;">
                <td> Rebecca </td>
                <td> Jones </td>
                <td> May 2 </td>
            </tr>
            <tr style="color:blue;">
                <td> Tony </td>
                <td> White </td>
                <td> April 14 </td>
            </tr>
            <tr style="color:purple;">
                <td> Jamie </td>
```

```
            <td> Parker </td>
            <td> August 27 </td>
        </tr>
    </table>
</body>
</html>
```

When you save it with the .html file extension and open it with your browser, it should look like this:

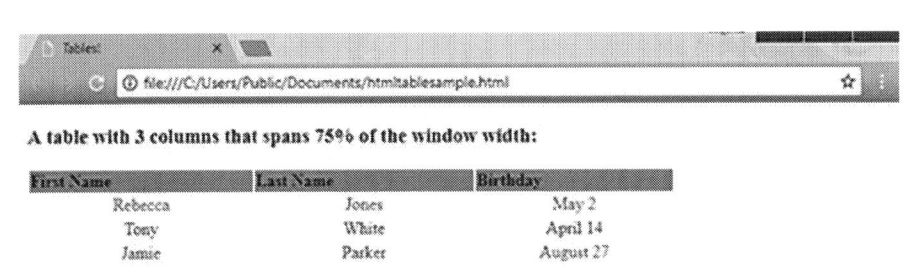

A table with 3 columns that spans 75% of the window width:

First Name	Last Name	Birthday
Rebecca	Jones	May 2
Tony	White	April 14
Jamie	Parker	August 27

If you'd like, you can add borders to your table elements using the **border** attribute. You can instruct these separate borders to mesh into one border with the **border-collapse** attribute:

```
<style>
    table, th, td {border: 1px solid black; border-collapse:collapse;}
</style>
```

You can also use the colspan and rowspan attributes to create cells that cover multiple columns or rows. For instance, if two individuals had the same birthday in the above example, you might want to display it like so:

```
<tr>
    <th> First Name </th>
    <th> Last Name </th>
    <th> Birthday </th>
</tr>
<tr>
```

```
            <td> Rebecca </td>
            <td> Jones </td>
            <td rowspan="2"> May 2 </td>
      </tr>
      <tr>
            <td> Tony </td>
            <td> White </td>
      </tr>
      <tr>
            <td> Jamie </td>
            <td> Parker </td>
            <td> August 27 </td>
      </tr>
```

Try it yourself! Copy and paste or manually type the following bit of HTML into your own text editor:

```
<!DOCTYPE html>
<html>
    <head>
            <title> Tables! </title>
            <style>
                    table, th, td {border: 1px solid black; border-collapse:collapse;}
                    th {text-align:left;}
                    td {text-align:center;}
            </style>
    </head>
    <body>
                    <h3> A table with 3 columns that uses the default width and colors: </h3>
            <table>
                    <tr>
                            <th> First Name </th>
```

```
                <th> Last Name </th>
                <th> Birthday </th>
        </tr>
        <tr>
                <td> Rebecca </td>
                <td> Jones </td>
                <td> May 2 </td>
        </tr>
        <tr>
                <td> Tony </td>
                <td> White </td>
                <td> April 14 </td>
        </tr>
        <tr>
                <td> Jamie </td>
                <td> Parker </td>
                <td> August 27 </td>
        </tr>
</table>

<h3> A table with 3 columns that spans 75% of the window width and uses defined colors: </h3>
<table style="width:75%">
        <tr style="background-color:grey;">
                <th> First Name </th>
                <th> Last Name </th>
                <th> Birthday </th>
        </tr>
        <tr style="color:green;">
                <td> Rebecca </td>
                <td> Jones </td>
                <td> May 2 </td>
        </tr>
        <tr style="color:blue;">
                <td> Tony </td>
```

```html
                <td> White </td>
                <td> April 14 </td>
        </tr>
        <tr style="color:purple;">
                <td> Jamie </td>
                <td> Parker </td>
                <td> August 27 </td>
        </tr>
</table>
```

<h3> A table with 3 columns that spans 75% of the window width and uses merged rows: </h3>
```html
<table style="width:75%">
        <tr>
                <th> First Name </th>
                <th> Last Name </th>
                <th> Birthday </th>
        </tr>
        <tr>
                <td> Rebecca </td>
                <td> Jones </td>
                <td rowspan="2"> May 2 </td>
        </tr>
        <tr>
                <td> Tony </td>
                <td> White </td>
        </tr>
        <tr>
                <td> Jamie </td>
                <td> Parker </td>
                <td> August 27 </td>
        </tr>
</table>
    </body>
</html>
```

Once you save this HTML with the .html extension and open it with a browser, your web page should look something like this:

A table with 3 columns that uses the default width and colors:

First Name	Last Name	Birthday
Rebecca	Jones	May 2
Tony	White	April 14
Jamie	Parker	August 27

A table with 3 columns that spans 75% of the window width and uses defined colors:

First Name	Last Name	Birthday
Rebecca	Jones	May 2
Tony	White	April 14
Jamie	Parker	August 27

A table with 3 columns that spans 75% of the window width and uses merged rows:

First Name	Last Name	Birthday
Rebecca	Jones	May 2
Tony	White	
Jamie	Parker	August 27

What other ways can I display my content?

In addition to lists and tables, you can also use HTML to format your text into block quotations, subscripts, superscripts, computer code, and even reversed text. Check out the following HTML to see how to use tags to format your page using these different techniques:

```
<!DOCTYPE html>
<html>
   <head>
           <title> Other Formats! </title>
   </head>
   <body>
           <h3> The following is a block quotation: </h3>
           <blockquote> This is a block quotation. Usually, browsers indent block quotations. You can use this tag when you want to quote long pieces of text from other sources. </blockquote>
           <h3> The following text contains subscript and superscript: </h3>
           <p> This paragraph uses <sub> subscript </sub> and <sup> superscript </sup> elements, which can be useful when working with math. </p>
           <h3> The following text is formatted to look like computer code: </h3>
           <code> If your page is relevant to programming, you might want to use this tag. </code>
           <h3> The following text is displayed right to left: </h3>
           <bdo dir="rtl"> Right to left! </bdo>
   </body>
</html>
```

Save the code prior in an HTML file and then open the file in your browser, and it should display like so:

The following is a block quotation:

> This is a block quotation. Usually, browsers indent block quotations. You can use this tag when you want to quote long pieces of text from other sources.

The following text contains subscript and superscript:

This paragraph uses $_{subscript}$ and ^{superscript} elements, which can be useful when working with math.

The following text is formatted to look like computer code:

```
If your page is relevant to programming, you might want to use this tag.
```

The following text is displayed right to left:

!tfel ot thgiR

Now that you've seen many of the different ways you can format and style the elements on your web page, try your hand at combining the techniques you've learned to further customize your page. Will you make a table with links? A page full of quotes? Interesting color coded informational tables? It's up to you!

Chapter 3

Creating HTML Forms And Handling Input

Oftentimes, when you are creating web pages, you are doing so with the intention of interacting with people who visit your page. One simple way to accomplish this is by incorporating an HTML form into your page to request input from your users.

What kinds of input can I accept from users?

Depending on the type of information you'd like to request from your users, you can incorporate a number of different input options into your forms. For instance, if you'd like a way for users to input their names, you could use a text input field. If you want users to choose from different available options, you could use radio buttons or a dropdown list of choices. Check out the options below for ways that you can use forms to request information from your users:

Text Fields: You can create a text field that is one line high through setting the input tag as **"text"** like so:

    Type your first name here:

    <input type="text"> </input>

Or, if you want to accept a larger quantity of text, like a message, you can create a text area using the <textarea> and </textarea> start and end tags.

Number Fields: You can create a field where users can input numerical values through setting the input tag as **"number"** like this:

>Please enter a number:
>
><input type="number"> </input>

A number field will not allow the user to enter in any characters besides numbers.

Password Fields: You can create a field where users can enter their password by setting the input tag as **"password"** like so:

>Type your password here:
>
><input type="password"> </input>

When a user types text into a password field, the characters are hidden for privacy.

Email Fields: You can create a field that accepts email addresses by setting the input tag as **"email"**, like this:

>Type your email address here:
>
><input type="email"> </input>

This field will require a user to enter a text value containing the @ symbol.

Radio Buttons: You can set the input tag to **"radio"** to create radio buttons like so:

><input type="radio" name="radiobuttons"> Option 1 </input>
><input type="radio" name="radiobuttons"> Option 2 </input>
><input type="radio" name="radiobuttons"> Option 3 </input>

Your user will only be able to select one of the available radio buttons at a time for radio buttons with the same **name** attribute value.

Checkboxes: You can create checkboxes for your forms by setting the input tag as **"checkbox"** as follows:

    <input type="checkbox"> I like coffee </input>
    <input type="checkbox"> I like tea </input>

Using checkboxes will let you users select none, some, or all of the options provided.

Drop-Down Lists: If you'd like to create a drop-down list with options for a user to choose from, you can do so by using the <select> and <option> tags like this:

    <select>
        <option> Square </option>
        <option> Circle </option>
        <option> Triangle </option>
        <option> Hexagon </option>
    </select>

Depending on the attributes you use, your user will be able to select either a single or multiple options from the drop-down list at a time.

Buttons: You can create a button that users can click on by setting the input tag to **"button"**. You can assign text to the button using the **value** attribute like so:

    <input type="button" value="I'm a button!"> </input>

Note: nothing will happen when you click this button as is; you will need to assign it an action when it is clicked using the **onclick** attribute, which you'll see in the next section.

Color Choosers: You can allow your users to select a color using a color picker by setting the input tag to **"color"** like this:

    Please choose your favorite color:

    <input type="color"> </input>

Date Selectors: You can allow your users to select a date from a calendar by setting the input tag to **"date"** like this:

> Please select your birthdate:
>
> <input type="date"> </input>

Range Sliders: Your users can select a relative value on a sliding scale with a range slider which you can create by setting the input tag to **"range"** like so:

> Cold
> <input type="range"> </input>
> Hot

Submit Buttons: The submit button sends the data from your form to a handler, which processes the data from the form. You can create a submit button by setting the input tag to **"submit"** like this:

> <input type="submit"> </input>

The submit button refers to the **action** attribute in the <form> start tag to know where to send the data, which is generally a page with a data processing script.

Reset Buttons: If you would like your users to be able to set all of the options in your form back to their original default values, you can incorporate a reset button by setting the input tag to **"reset"** like so:

> <input type="reset"> </input>

Each form you create will use the <form> and </form> start and end tags to specify where the form begins and ends. This allows certain elements to know what to send when the form is submitted and enables you to have multiple forms on one page which can be submitted individually. Copy and paste or manually type in the following HTML into your text editor to see how different basic form elements appear in by default:

```html
<!DOCTYPE html>
<html>
    <head>
        <title> Forms! </title>
    </head>
    <body>
        <h2> A form with multiple input types: </h2>
        <form>
            <h3> A text field: </h3>
            Type your name below:
            <br>
            <input type="text"> </input>

            <h3> A number field: </h3>
            Please enter your favorite number:
            <br>
            <input type="number"> </input>

            <h3> A password field: </h3>
            Type your password below:
            <br>
            <input type="password"> </input>

            <h3> An email field: </h3>
            Type your email below:
            <br>
            <input type="email"> </input>

            <h3> Radio buttons: </h3>
            <input type="radio" name="radiobuttons"> Option 1 </input>
            <input type="radio" name="radiobuttons"> Option 2 </input>
            <input type="radio" name="radiobuttons"> Option 3 </input>
```

```html
<h3> Checkboxes: </h3>
<input type="checkbox"> I like coffee </input>
<input type="checkbox"> I like tea </input>

<h3> A drop-down list: </h3>
<select>
        <option> Square </option>
        <option> Circle </option>
        <option> Triangle </option>
        <option> Hexagon </option>
</select>

<h3> A color picker: </h3>
Please choose your favorite color:
<br>
<input type="color"> </input>

<h3> A date picker: </h3>
Please select your birthdate:
<br>
<input type="date"> </input>

<h3> A slider: </h3>
Cold
 <input type="range"> </input>
Hot

<h3> Standard, submit, and reset buttons: </h3>
<input type="button" value="I'm a button!">
</input>
<input type="submit"> </input>
<input type="reset"> </input>
        </form>
    </body>
</html>
```

When you save this HTML in a file using the .html extension and then open it with a browser, your page should look something like this:

A form with multiple input types:

A text field:

Please enter your name:

A number field:

Please enter your favorite number:

A password field:

Please enter your password:

An email field:

Please enter your email address:

Radio buttons:

○ Option 1 ○ Option 2 ○ Option 3

Checkboxes:

☐ I like coffee ☐ I like tea

A drop-down list:

[Square ▼]

A color picker:

Please choose your favorite color:

A date picker:

Please select your birthdate:
[mm/dd/yyyy]

A slider:

Cold ———◻——— Hot

Standard, submit, and reset buttons:

[I'm a button!] [Submit] [Reset]

How can I customize the forms on my web page?

Just like you can use attributes to change certain aspects of the text and images on your page, you can use attributes to enhance the elements in your forms. Some of the most common attributes you might use when creating forms are the following:

name: You should use the **name** attribute to assign a reference name to elements or groups of elements. This will enable other elements to interact with the element and form handlers to know what each piece of input data should refer to. Certain elements need to have a **name** attribute value assigned in order to work correctly like the radio buttons in the last section. You should use descriptive values to define this attribute.

value: The **value** attribute allows you to assign default values to the elements in your forms. For instance, you could have a word or phrase populate in a text field when your form is generated, or you could have a radio button pre-selected.

required: This attribute signifies that the field is required and that the form cannot be submitted without a value entered.

disabled: This attribute signifies that the current field should be disabled and unable to accept any input from a user.

max: The value for this attribute will define the maximum value that the input field is able to accept.

maxlength: Similarly to the **max** attribute, the value of the **maxlength** attribute defines how many characters an input field is able to accept from the user.

min: The value for this attribute will define the minimum value that the input field is able to accept.

size: The value assigned to the **size** attribute defines how many characters wide an input field should be.

Other attributes only pertain to specific input types. Read through the HTML below to view some examples of attributes used for form elements:

```
<!DOCTYPE html>
<html>
  <head>
      <title> Forms! </title>
  </head>
  <body>
      <h2> A form with multiple input types: </h2>
      <form>
          <h3> A text field with a specified size, a default value, and a maximum input length: </h3>
          Please enter your first name:
          <br>
          <input type="text" value="Mario" maxlength="10" size="12" name="firstname"> </input>

          <h3> A disabled text field: </h3>
          Please enter your last name:
          <br>
          <input type="text" name="lastname" disabled> </input>

          <h3> A large text area: </h3>
          Please write a message:
          <br>
          <textarea rows="5" cols="35" name="msgbox"> Some default text! </textarea>

          <h3> A number field with a maximum accepted value of 10: </h3>
          Please enter your favorite number less than or equal to 10:
```

```
<br>
<input     type="number"     max="10"
name="favnum"> </input>
```

A number field with a specified step value:

```
Please enter a multiple of 5:
<br>
<input     type="number"     step="5"
name="favnum"> </input>
```

A long password field:

```
Please enter your password:
<br>
<input   type="password"   name="password"
size="60"> </input>
```

An email field that requires input:

```
Please enter your email address:
<br>
<input type="email" name="email" required>
</input>
```

Radio buttons with one checked by default:

```
<input   type="radio"   name="textstyle">   <b>
bold </b> </input>
<input type="radio" name="textstyle" checked>
<i> italics </i> </input>
<input type="radio" name="textstyle"> <mark>
highlighted </mark> </input>
```

Checkboxes that are checked by default:

```
<input type="checkbox" name="beverages" checked> I like coffee </input>
<input type="checkbox" name="beverages" checked> I like tea </input>
```

A drop-down list that allows users to pick one option, with one selected by default:

```
<select name="ashape">
    <option> Square </option>
    <option> Circle </option>
    <option selected> Triangle </option>
    <option> Hexagon </option>
</select>
```

A drop-down list that shows 2 options at a time and allows users to pick multiple options using the ctrl key:

```
<select name="shapes" size="2" multiple>
    <option> Square </option>
    <option> Circle </option>
    <option> Triangle </option>
    <option> Hexagon </option>
</select>
```

A color picker:

Please choose your favorite color:
```
<br>
<input type="color" name="favcolor"> </input>
```

A date picker with date restrictions:

Please select a date in 2000:
```
<br>
<input type="date" name="somedate" min="2000-01-01" max="2000-12-31"> </input>
```

```
            <h3> A slider set to the minimum value by
            default: </h3>
            Cold
            <input type="range" value="0"> </input>
            Hot

            <h3> Standard, submit, and reset buttons: </h3>
            <input type="button" onclick="alert('You
            clicked me!')" value="I'm a button!"> </input>
            <input type="submit" value="Submit form!">
            </input>
            <input type="reset" value="Reset form!">
            </input>
        </form>
    </body>
</html>
```

Save this HTML with a .html extension and open it with your browser. It should look like this:

A form with multiple input types:

A text field with a specified size, a default value, and a maximum input length:

Please enter your first name:
`Mario`

A disabled text field:

Please enter your last name:
`[disabled]`

A large text area:

Please write a message:
```
Some default text!
```

A number field with a maximum accepted value of 10:

Please enter your favorite number less than or equal to 10:

A number field with a specified step value:

Please enter a multiple of 5:

A long password field:

Please enter your password:

An email field that requires input:

Please enter your email address:

Radio buttons with one checked by default:

○ **bold** ● *italics* ○ <mark>highlighted</mark>

Checkboxes that are checked by default:

☑ I like coffee ☑ I like tea

A drop-down list that allows users to pick one option, with one selected by default:

`Triangle ▼`

A drop-down list that shows 2 options at a time and allows users to pick multiple options using the ctrl key:

`Square`
`Circle`

A color picker:

Please choose your favorite color:
`[■]`

A date picker with date restrictions:

Please select a date in 2000:
`mm/dd/2000`

A slider set to the minimum value by default:

Cold `[○────────]` Hot

Standard, submit, and reset buttons:

`[I'm a button!]` `[Submit form!]` `[Reset form!]`

62

Great job! Now, play around with the elements of your form. What happens if you try to enter a value of 11 into the number field with a maximum value of 10? What about if you try to type more than 10 characters into the first text field? See how you can manipulate the different elements of your HTML form in ways that can be useful for your web page!

Chapter 4

HTML And CSS

In previous examples, you learned how to define the style for your elements in 2 different ways: in the start tag for the element itself, or within the <style> element within the <head> element of your HTML file. In doing so, you were actually using CSS already using inline and internal techniques. Next, let's look at how to define styles for your page and its elements externally using a separate CSS file.

What is CSS?

The initials CSS literally stand for the words Cascading Style Sheets. With CSS, you can define the style for a specific element, a type of element, or for your entire webpage easily and efficiently. Although you can use CSS within your HTML document or even within an individual element, perhaps the most efficient way to use CSS is by defining the styles for your website within an external document saved with a .css extension. By doing so, you enable yourself to alter the appearance of your entire website by changing a single file instead of individual pages or elements.

An external style sheet cannot contain any HTML code. The contents of your external CSS file will resemble the contents of the <style> element within the <head> element of an HTML document. If you've been following along with the examples in the previous chapters, this should look familiar to you! A simple .css file might look like this:

```css
body {
    background-color: black;
}
h2 {
    color: white;
}
p {
    background-color: white;
    color: blue;
    font-family: courier;
}
```

Type the CSS from above into your text editor and save it with a .css extension as something like styles.css. To use the .css file with an HTML document, you will first need to define a link to the .css file within the <head> element of your HTML. Let's use a simple HTML example:

```html
<!DOCTYPE html>
<html>
    <head>
        <title> CSS! </title>
        <link rel="stylesheet" href="styles.css"> </link>
    </head>
    <body>
        <h2> This heading uses the styles defined in your external CSS file! </h2>
        <p> This paragraph uses the styles defined in your external CSS file! </p>
    </body>
</html>
```

Save this HTML with a .html file extension in the same folder as your styles.css file. When you open the .html file using your browser, you should be able to see a heading and paragraph displayed using the styles you defined in your CSS file:

> **This heading uses the styles defined in your external CSS file!**
>
> This paragraph uses the styles defined in your external CSS file!

How can CSS enhance my web page?

You've already used CSS throughout this tutorial to style the elements of your webpage. By using an external .css style sheet, you can make the process of styling your webpage even simpler by containing all of your style rules in one place. You can use your style sheet to define how different types of elements should each be displayed in terms of sizes, fonts, colors, outlines, margins, and alignment, and then link to the same .css file from multiple HTML documents. Even if your website has 100 pages, you'll only have to write your CSS once!

In addition to assigning styles to specific element types like headings and paragraphs, you can also assign unique styles to individual elements using CSS. Let's take a look at a couple of different ways we can do this. The first way uses the id attribute within the start tag of an element.

For instance, let's slightly alter the HTML and CSS examples from the last section:

```
<!DOCTYPE html>
<html>
   <head>
        <title> CSS! </title>
        <link rel="stylesheet" href="styles.css"> </link>
   </head>
   <body>
        <h2> This is a normal h2 heading </h2>
        <p> This is a normal paragraph </p>
        <p id="special"> Example of a special id </p>
   </body>
</html>
```

Now, update your styles.css file to the following:

```css
body {
    background-color: black;
}
h2 {
    color: white;
}
p {
    background-color: white;
    color: blue;
    font-family: courier;
}
#special {
    color: green;
}
```

Upon opening your file with your web browser, you should be able to see that the element with the **"special"** id uses the style defined by **#special** in the .css file:

```
This is a normal h2 heading
This is a normal paragraph
This is a paragraph with a special id
```

Note: no 2 elements should be given the same id within a single page, so this method should only be used to alter individual elements.

Alternatively, you can use classes to style subsets of element types with CSS. For example, you could divide your paragraphs into normal and special classes and then use CSS to assign a different color to the special paragraph class. Copy and paste or manually type the following CSS code within your editor of choice and save it as styles.css:

```css
body {
    background-color: black;
}
h2 {
    color: white;
}
p {
    background-color: white;
    color: blue;
    font-family: courier;
}
p.special {
    background-color: grey;
    color: aqua;
}
```

Now copy and paste or manually type the following HTML into your text editor:

```html
<!DOCTYPE html>
<html>
    <head>
        <title> CSS! </title>
        <link rel="stylesheet" href="styles.css"> </link>
    </head>
    <body>
        <h2> This is a heading </h2>
        <p> This is a normal paragraph </p>
        <p class="special"> Example of a special class </p>
    </body>
</html>
```

Once you save the HTML document and then open it with a browser, your page should resemble the following:

This is a heading

This is a normal paragraph

This is a paragraph with a special id

Since multiple elements can have the same class value, you can use this method to assign specific styles to large subsets of element types. Even better, you can update the style of all of the elements with the same class name by simply updating your .css file—there's no need to update each individual element inline!

To get an idea of how to further use an external style sheet to define how your HTML page is displayed, copy and paste or manually type the following CSS code within your editor of choice and save it as styles.css:

```
body {
    background-color: aqua;
    font-family: courier;
}
h1 {
}
h2 {
    color: purple;
    text-align: center;
}
h3 {
    color: green;
    font-family: verdana;
}
h4 {
    color: grey;
    font-family: times;
    text-align: right;
}
h5 {
    background-color: black;
    color: white;
```

```css
}
h6 {
    text-align: center;
}
h6.error {
    color: red;
    font-weight: bold;
}
p {
    background-color: white;
    color: blue;
    font-family: verdana;
}
p.fancy {
    background-color: grey;
    color: aqua;
    font-family: cursive;
}
p.important {
    font-weight: bold;
    font-size: 200%;
    text-transform: capitalize;
    text-align: center;
}
p.right {
    text-align: right;
}
#special {
    font-size: 300%;
    background-color: aqua;
    color: green;
}
img {
    background-color: black;
}
```

```css
img.big {
    width: 100%;
    height: 100%;
}
img.bordered {
    border-color: white;
    border-width: medium;
    border-style: solid;
}
img.dashborder {
    border-width: medium;
    border-color: white;
    border-style: dashed;
}
```

Then, copy and paste or manually type the following HTML into your text editor:

```html
<!DOCTYPE html>
<html>
    <head>
            <title> CSS! </title>
            <link rel="stylesheet" href="styles.css"> </link>
    </head>
    <body>
            <h1> This is an h1 heading </h1>
            <h2> This is an h2 heading </h2>
            <h3> This is an h3 heading </h3>
            <h4> This is an h4 heading </h4>
            <h5> This is an h5 heading </h5>
            <h6> This is an h6 heading </h6>
            <h6 class="error"> This is an h6 error heading </h6>
            <p> This is a paragraph </p>
            <p class="fancy"> This is a fancy paragraph </p>
```

```
          <p class="important"> This is an important paragraph
</p>
          <p class="right"> This is a right aligned paragraph </p>
          <p id="special"> Example of a special id </p>
          <p class="fancy"> Another fancy paragraph! </p>
          <img src="shapes.png">
          <br>
          <img src="shapes.png" class="big">
          <br>
          <img src="shapes.png" class="bordered">
          <br>
          <img src="shapes.png" class="dashborder">
     </body>
</html>
```

Save both files in the same folder along with an image called shapes.png and then open the HTML document with your web browser. The elements of your page will be aligned, sized, colored, and bordered in the ways that you specified in your .css file!

Now that you've got a basic idea of how you are able to use external CSS files to specify different styles for the elements in your HTML documents, take some time to practice. The previous example used a .css file to define styles for headings, paragraphs, and images. See if you can apply the same techniques to style other elements like links, tables, lists, or form elements. You'll be efficiently making unique web pages with custom styles in no time!

Chapter 5

Using Div Elements

In HTML, and especially with the advent of HTML5, there are many different dividing elements one can use in order to break your document up into several different sections, all of which have their own specialty but function in similar ways.

Remember, HTML is ultimately a *markup* language. It's intended to take text and present it in a certain way using codified standards. This means that, to one extent or another, the language itself should ideally be easy to understand. In order to aid in making HTML easier to understand, certain conventions have been created that allow people to write better markup. Among these are these new divider elements.

The oldest divider element, and in fact one which has been around for quite a while, is the *div* element. The div element normally will take either an *ID* or a *class* (or both). These are defined in the markup for the div element.

We've already talked about both of these in passing but since IDs and classes are actually a concept that you're going to run into fairly often when you're working with HTML and CSS, it's worth taking a second to really start to understand what they are and what the difference is between them. They are different and you can absolutely use both in order to mark a single element.

IDs and classes are similar but functionally different in a fundamental way. IDs serve as a means for designating a single element. In this way, an ID is an identifier, hence the name "ID." You cannot have two elements with the same identifier. All identifiers must be unique.

Classes are parallel to identifiers. They allow you to designate a single *type* of element. So, if you wanted every element of your site that was designated as a *content-box* to have a drop shadow, you could do so by setting these to be of the class *content-box*.

Something may be designated through both an ID and a class. If you were to do this, then it would take the style properties from both (something we'll talk about more in-depth in the book specifically geared at CSS). If they both have a similar property, like border-color for instance, then the class definition will be superseded by the ID definition.

IDs and classes can be written in your markup like so:

```
<div id="idName" class="className">
    <!-- content -->
</div>
```

Note that you don't necessarily have to have both of these. You can have only one and that would be perfectly fine. You also don't have to have either of these. However, if you decide to use these, then that will give you a way to define further things for these markup elements both within your CSS and within any JavaScript or PHP code that you write. As a result, getting into the habit of using these is extremely important. You can use them with pretty much any element that you want to style, but there is a way to use them excessively and in places where they don't really belong, so only use them when they have a specific purpose within the context of your code.

Another divider element that you should know is the *nav* element. The nav element is intended to give you an easy way to mark out where the navigation bar in your code is. Like so:

```
<nav>
    <a href=""> Link 1 </a>
    <a href=""> Link 2 </a>
    <a href=""> Link 3 </a>
</nav>
```

One can also try the section element, which will allow one to break their code into sections. This is functionally similar to the *div* element, but the language is a bit clearer. Where div can be used for generally any division, the *section* element is particularly useful within the context of modern web design where one-page designs that are broken into singular sections in the code are the modus operandi.

While we're discussing dividing elements, it's also important that you understand how they work in the context of linking back to your site. You can actually use identifiers in order to link to a certain place on your page. For example, if you were to have a div called "endOfPage" by an ID, you could link to the page in a manner such that clicking the link would take you to the start of that division. Like so:

<a href="#endOfPage"> Go to the End of the Page. </a>

This is especially useful when you're linking within your own document and working with the aforementioned single-page designs.

You refer to identifiers with a pound sign and to classes using a period, just for the record.

Another important sectional divider that you should probably know is the *footer* element. This allows you to designate in clear language the *footer* of a given page. This works just like the nav, section, and div elements do.

With that, we've covered most of the major division elements that you're going to need to get started with HTML. You can style according to these division markers and then have a very expressive markup document that will clearly show what is what and where.

Conclusion

Thank you again for purchasing *HTML: Basic Fundamental Guide for Beginners*, and congratulations on making it to the end! Hopefully, you've gained some insight into how HTML uses tags, elements, and attributes to tell a browser how to display a web page, and had some fun designing your very own web page from scratch.

The next step is to let yourself get creative. Have an idea for a cool new web page? Try using your new HTML skills to bring it to life! As with any other skill, if you really want to continue progressing with HTML, the best way is to practice using it every chance you get—there are a ton of websites out there just waiting to be made, and that means a ton of opportunities for you.

Finally, if you found this book useful as you began on your HTML journey, please take a moment to review it on Amazon. Thank you, good luck, and enjoy your new website!

CSS

Basic Fundamental Guide for Beginners

Introduction

Congratulations on purchasing *CSS: Basic Fundamental Guide For Beginners* and thank you for doing so! Whether you're interested in learning CSS to enhance a personal website or you'd just like to gain a better understanding of how your browser does what it does. This book is a great starting point. With its many examples and simple to understand explanations, you'll soon be on your way to creating unique web pages that function smoothly and efficiently!

Before diving into this book, a basic idea of HTML is a plus and how to use it to create a simple web page. Combine that knowledge with an editor and a browser and you're ready to get started! Over the course of this book, you'll not only learn the art of using CSS selectors in making our HTML web pages more interactive, you'll also discover techniques for creating beautiful page layouts. When it comes to interacting with users, having an approachable and easy-to-use website is crucial. By the end of this book, you can be confident that your web pages are just as simple to navigate as they are appealing to view.

There are many books available on this subject, so thanks again for choosing this one. Good luck, and have fun taking off with CSS!

Chapter 1

Taking Off With CSS

If you have ever written HTML to create a web page previously, it is highly likely that you've also used CSS. CSS stands literally for Cascading Style Sheets, and it is used in web pages alongside HTML to define page styles and layouts. Need to change the default font of a paragraph? Wish that picture had a border? Would a cool animation really bring your page to life? You can do all of that using CSS!

With the examples here, just get one text editor (like Notepad or TextEdit) to write some HTML and CSS and a browser (like Google Chrome, Internet Explorer, or Mozilla Firefox) to view what you've written.

How do CSS and HTML work together?

Generally speaking, your web browser will use the rules that you set within your CSS to determine how to display a web page. An HTML file will provide the content and define the content's type, and a CSS file will assign different styles to those different content types. CSS uses what are called properties and selectors to assign these styles. A property can be something like an element's size or color. A selector is what CSS uses to refer to an element or group of elements in order to assign them a style.

You can contain all of the rules for how to display the elements in your HTML document within a separate file called a stylesheet. A stylesheet will have a .css file extension, and you will link to it within the <head> element of your HTML file. For instance, consider the following HTML:

```html
<!DOCTYPE html>
<html>
    <head>
        <title>A CSS Example!</title>
    </head>
    <body>
        <h1>A big important heading</h1>
        <p>An ordinary paragraph</p>
    </body>
</html>
```

If you save the above HTML in a file with a .html extension and then open it using a browser, it won't look very impressive -- just black text on a white background. However, you can change that with a little bit of CSS. Take a look at the following:

```css
h1 {
    background-color: red;
    color: white;
    border: 2px dashed blue;
}
p {
    background-color: grey;
    color: aqua;
}
```

Save this CSS in a file called styles.css. Now, we'll just have to add one line into the previous HTML example, thereby connecting CSS stylesheet with the HTML file. In the <head> element, insert a <link> element as follows:

```html
<!DOCTYPE html>
<html>
    <head>
            <title>A CSS Example!</title>
            <link rel="stylesheet" href="styles.css">
    </head>
    <body>
            <h1>A big important heading</h1>
            <p>An ordinary paragraph</p>
    </body>
</html>
```

Save this HTML with a .html extension in the same folder where you just saved styles.css. Now when you open your HTML using your browser, it will look a little more interesting:

A big important heading

An ordinary paragraph

So what did we just do? In our .css file, we defined two rules. Both rules start with a selector and then contain declarations, which define the values for certain properties. The selector for the first rule is **h1**, and the rule contains three declarations: the first declaration generates red background color, white color emanates from the next, and the third declaration creates a dashed blue border around the element. The selector for the second rule is **p**, and it contains two declarations: the first declaration sets the background color to grey, and the second declaration sets the text color to aqua. These rules will apply to every element in your HTML file that use <h1> or <p> tags.

How can I use CSS with my HTML?

In the last section, you put some CSS into a separate file from your HTML document and then linked to that file in order to use the styles it defined. When you use CSS in this manner, it's called an external stylesheet. In most cases, this is the method that you should use when styling your websites. Not only does this method allow you to efficiently organize all the styling rules for your web page in one place, it also allows you to use the same rules for multiple pages by linking to the same .css file from multiple .html files. That means that even if your website contains 100 pages, you can control the style for all of them just by altering a single .css file!

If for some reason you don't want to use an external stylesheet, you have a couple of other options for using CSS to style your HTML documents. Before we look at those options, first take a moment to remember how the HTML and CSS looked using the external stylesheet method.

Some HTML:

```
<!DOCTYPE html>
<html>
   <head>
         <title>A CSS Example!</title>
         <link rel="stylesheet" href="styles.css">
   </head>
   <body>
         <h1>A big important heading</h1>
         <p>An ordinary paragraph</p>
         <h2>A less important heading to introduce a list</h2>
         <ul>
               A list of assorted objects:
               <li>a hairbrush</li>
               <li>a skeleton key</li>
               <li>a cat</li>
               <li>a gaming console</li>
               <li>a pancake</li>
         <ul>
   </body>
</html>
```
Some CSS:

```css
h1 {
    background-color: red;
    color: white;
    border: 2px dashed blue;
}
h2 {
    background-color: purple;
    color: yellow;
}
p {
    background-color: grey;
    color: aqua;
}
ul {
    text-decoration: underline;
    border: 1px solid green;
}
li {
    text-decoration: bold;
}
```

The first alternative to using an external stylesheet that we'll take a look at is called an internal stylesheet. Instead of placing a <link> element within the <head> element of your HTML document, you'll instead use a <style> element to contain the CSS declarations. To create the same page as the example above using an internal stylesheet, your HTML document would look something like this:

```html
<!DOCTYPE html>
<html>
    <head>
        <title>A CSS Example!</title>
        <style>
            h1 {
                background-color: red;
```

```
        color: white;
        border: 2px dashed blue;
}
h2 {
        background-color: purple;
        color: yellow;
}
p {
        background-color: grey;
        color: aqua;
}
ul {
        text-decoration: underline;
        border: 1px solid green;
}
li {
        text-decoration: bold;
}
            </style>
    </head>
    <body>
        <h1>A big important heading</h1>
        <p>An ordinary paragraph</p>
        <h2>A less important heading to introduce a list</h2>
        <ul>
            A list of assorted objects:
            <li>a hairbrush</li>
            <li>a skeleton key</li>
            <li>a cat</li>
            <li>a gaming console</li>
            <li>a pancake</li>
        <ul>
    </body>
</html>
```

This method has the benefit of containing all of the styling information you need in the same document as your HTML. Changing the styles within the <style> element will apply them to the <h1> and <p> elements throughout your .html document. However, if you want to create multiple pages with the same style rules, you'll have to put the CSS into each file individually. Then, if you decide you want to change something, you'll have to change it in multiple files.

A third option for applying CSS to you HTML document is via inline styles. Inline styles only affect a single HTML element, and they are defined within the **style** attribute in the start tag of an element. To create the same page as above using inline styles, you would have to do the following:

```
<!DOCTYPE html>
<html>
    <head>
        <title>A CSS Example!</title>
    </head>
    <body>
        <h1 style="background-color: red; color: white; border: 2px dashed blue;">A big important heading</h1>
        <p style="background-color: grey; color: aqua;">An ordinary paragraph</p>
    </body>
        <h2 style="background-color: purple; color: yellow">A less important heading to introduce a list</h2>
        <ul style="text-decoration: underline; border: 1px solid green;" >
            A list of assorted objects:
            <li style="text-decoration: bold;">a hairbrush</li>
            <li style="text-decoration: bold;">a skeleton key</li>
            <li style="text-decoration: bold;">a cat</li>
```

```
            <li    style="text-decoration:   bold;">a   gaming
console</li>
            <li      style="text-decoration:       bold;">a
pancake</li>
        <ul>
</html>
```

Although this might be a reasonable option in certain restrictive circumstances, it is generally not a good idea to use inline styles. If you decide to change any of the styles on your website, you won't just have to update each affected page -- you'll have to update each affected *element*. Additionally, having the styles defined within the start tag of each element tends to clutter up your HTML file and make it harder to read and understand.

How should I format my CSS?

You've already seen a couple of simple examples of how to properly format your CSS in the previous sections. Take a look at the following components to gain a better understanding of CSS syntax:

Property: A property is an identifier that is used to indicate what feature of an element you want to style. Properties are descriptive and meant to be easy for a human to read and understand. Some examples of properties include size, font, color, and border. There are over 300 properties available to use in CSS! CSS properties are case sensitive and they all use US spelling -- color doesn't work, but color does.

Value: A value is assigned to a property to define what its specific style should be. A color property could have a value of blue or red, for instance. The available values depend on which property they're defining. Like properties, values are case sensitive.

Declaration: A CSS declaration is the pairing of a property with a value. A declaration is formatted as follows, with the property first, a colon, and then the value:

color: blue;

background-color: purple;

width: 100%;

font-family: courier;

It's worth noting here that not every value is valid for every property. Each property has its own list of acceptable values. If you try to use an invalid property or value in your declaration, the browser will simply ignore the whole declaration.

Declaration block: A declaration block contains zero or more CSS declarations. The declaration blocks are contained in {} brackets and separated by semicolons. The final declaration in a declaration block doesn't need to end with a semicolon, but that is better to ensure consistency:

```
{color: blue;
    background-color: aqua;
    border-left: 1px dashed green;
    width: 100%;
    text-decoration: underline;
}
```

Ruleset: A ruleset or rule is the pairing of a declaration block with a CSS selector or group of selectors. This pairing is accomplished simply by placing the selector or group of selectors before the opening {bracket of the declaration block. Each selector in a group of selectors should be separated by a comma:

```
h1 {
    background-color: black;
    color: white;
    font-family: courier;
}
```

```
h2, p {
    background-color: grey;
    color: aqua;
    font-family: verdana;
}
```

If any of the selectors in a group of selectors is invalid, the browser will skip over it. However, the browser will still apply the styles set in the declaration block to the remaining selectors in the group.

In addition to understanding and properly formatting your CSS rules, it is also generally a good idea to use whitespace to your advantage within your .css files. Although it isn't necessary to create a functioning web page, using line breaks, tabs, and spaces in your file can make it readable and simple to alter if the need arises. For instance, this CSS:

```
h1 {
background-color:red;
color:white;
font-family: courier;
border:2px dashed blue;
}
p {
background-color:grey;
font-family: verdana;
color:aqua;
}
```
and this CSS:
h1{background-color:red;color:white;font-family:courier;border:2px dashed blue;}p{background-color:grey;font-family:verdana;color:aqua;}

will both define the same styles for your web pages. However, it is much easier to see and understand what is being done in the first example, and it would be much easier to make any changes if needed.

Chapter 2

Using CSS Selectors

In the last chapter, you had a chance to work with some basic CSS examples, and you learned that one or more selectors should come before a declaration block. Now, let's take a look at some of the different selector types and how they can be used to apply styles to your web pages:

Simple Selectors

A simple selector is used to refer to a single or multiple elements based on their ID, their class, or their type. A simple selector could look like any one of the following:

>p
>
>h4
>
>ol
>
>.someclass
>
>.important
>
>p.error
>
>#q1
>
>#input4
>
>*

The first kind of simple selector is very common and is called a type selector or an element selector. Type selectors are not case sensitive, and they are a simple way to refer to all of the elements of the same type within an HTML document, like all the type 1 headings or all the ordered lists. For the following HTML:

```
<!DOCTYPE html>
<html>
   <head>
          <title>CSS Type Selectors</title>
          <link rel="stylesheet" href="styles.css">
   </head>
   <body>
          <p>A paragraph with a defined color and background color</p>
          <ol>
                 A list with a border:
                 <li>square</li>
                 <li>circle</li>
                 <li>triangle</li>
          </ol>
   </body>
</html>
```

the following CSS uses the type selectors **p** and **ol** to style the <p> and <ol> elements:

```
p {
   background-color: blue;
   color: yellow;
   font-family: courier;
   text-decoration: bold;
}
ol {
   border: 1px solid green;
}
```

Another simple selector is the class selector. Instead of using the element type, the class selector uses a class name to refer to an element. In the .css file, the class selector is a period followed by the class name. In the .html file, the class name is written in the **class** attribute within an element's start tag. For example, for the following HTML:

```
<!DOCTYPE html>
<html>
   <head>
        <title>CSS Class Selectors</title>
        <link rel="stylesheet" href="styles.css">
   </head>
   <body>
       <ul>
            A list with items of different classes:
            <li class="shape first important">square</li>
            <li class="shape second important">circle</li>
            <li class="shape third">triangle</li>
       </ul>
   </body>
</html>
```

the following CSS uses the .shape, .first, .second, .third, and .important class selectors to style the items in the list. An element can have multiple classes, and it will use the styles assigned to all of its classes:

```
.shape {
   background-color: red;
   color: aqua;
}
.first {
   text-decoration: underline;
}
.second {
}
.third {
```

```
        font-family: courier;
}
.important {
        font-weight: bold;
}
```

The resulting list will look like so:

A list with items of different classes:
* square
* circle
* triangle

You can also use class selectors such as **p.error** or **p.valid** to refer to classes within a certain type of element. In this way, you could set a style for the error class that displays differently when it is a <p> element as opposed to a <div> or another type of element.

The third kind of simple selector is the ID selector. Similar to a class selector, an id selector refers to an id that is defined within the start tag of an element. However, while multiple elements can have the same class, only one element can have anID. If you attempt to assign the same id to multiple elements, you might encounter errors, or the browser might only accept the first instance. Take a look at the following HTML:

```
<!DOCTYPE html>
<html>
    <head>
            <title>CSS Class Selectors</title>
            <link rel="stylesheet" href="styles.css">
    </head>
    <body>
            <p id="george">George likes the color blue.</p>
            <p id="amy">Amy likes green.</p>
    </body>
</html>
```

and the following CSS:

```css
#george {
color: blue;
}
#amy {
color: green;
}
```

In the above example, you can see that ID selectors are written using the # symbol followed by the id value. Any element can be assigned a unique id within its start tag.

The final kind of simple selector that we will cover in this book is called the universal selector, which is simply written as the * symbol. The universal selector applies the styles defined in its declaration block to every element on the page. It is very uncommon to have a situation in which you should use the universal selector, and it can cause large web pages to have significantly poorer performance. A simple example could use the following HTML:

```html
<!DOCTYPE html>
<html>
   <head>
        <title>CSS Class Selectors</title>
        <link rel="stylesheet" href="styles.css">
   </head>
   <body>
        <h1>A large and important heading</h1>
        <p>A regular paragraph with some <b>bold</b>, <i>italicized</i>, and <u>underlined</u> elements.</p>
   </body>
</html>
```

and the following CSS:
```css
* {
```

```
    border: 1px double black;
    color: purple;
}
```

to create a page that looks like this:

> # A large and important heading
> A regular paragraph with some **bold**, *italicized*, and <u>underlined</u> elements.

Attribute Selectors

A somewhat more complex kind of selector is called an attribute selector, and it works by matching the value of an element's attribute. The attributes are contained within the start tag of an element in the .html file and are written in [] brackets in the .css stylesheet. For instance, take a look at the following HTML:

```
<!DOCTYPE html>
<html>
    <head>
        <title>CSS Class Selectors</title>
        <link rel="stylesheet" href="styles.css">
    </head>
    <body>
        A list of assorted things:
        <ul>
            <li thing-category="shape" thing-color="blue">square</li>
            <li thing-category="number" thing-color="none">four</li>
            <li thing-category="number" thing-color="none">17</li>
```

```html
            <li    thing-category="shape"    thing-color="green">circle</li>
            <li    thing-category="animal"   thing-color="white">bunny</li>
        </ul>
    </body>
</html>
```

and the following CSS:

```css
[thing-category] {
    background-color: aqua;
}
[thing-category=shape] {
    text-decoration: bold;
}
[thing-color] {
    color: red;
}
[thing-color=blue] {
    color: blue;
}
[thing-color=green] {
    color: green;
}
```

When viewed with a browser, your page should look similar to this:

A list of assorted things:

- square
- four
- 17
- circle
- bunny

In the above example, you can see how you can use attribute selectors in a couple of different ways. If you only list the attribute as the selector, the corresponding declaration block applies the contained styles. It does this to all, irrespective of the attribute value. On the other hand, if you list both an attribute and a value as the selector, the styles in the declaration block are only applied to elements that have that attribute set to that value.

Multiple Selectors

If you would like to use the same styles for more than one set of elements, you can pair multiple selectors with the same declaration block by separating them with commas. For example, if you use the following HTML:

```
<!DOCTYPE html>
<html>
   <head>
        <title>CSS Class Selectors</title>
        <link rel="stylesheet" href="styles.css">
   </head>
   <body>
        <h1>A big and important heading</h1>
        <h2>A less important heading</h2>
        <h3>An even less important heading</h3>
        <h4>A somewhat unimportant heading</h4>
        <h5>An even more unimportant heading</h5>
        <h6>A small and very unimportant heading</h6>
   </body>
</html>
```

with the following CSS:

```
h1, h3, h5 {
    background-color: grey;
}
```

```
h2, h4, h6 {
    color: blue;
}
```

your output will look something like this:

A big and important heading

A less important heading

An even less important heading

A somewhat unimportant heading

An even more unimportant heading

A small and very unimportant heading

Great! You now have an idea of how to use some common and useful selectors to apply custom styles to elements and groups of elements. Play around with the techniques you just learned. Can you figure out how to assign the same style to a class and an id without rewriting the declaration block? How does an element display if you assign different values to the same property within different declaration blocks? What happens if an element is nested within another element? Set up these scenarios in your text editor and find out!

Chapter 3

CSS Layout Basics

In the last chapters, you've had the opportunity to use CSS rules to define the styles for elements in your HTML documents. CSS doesn't just define appearance attributes like colors and borders, however. It is also a valuable tool in deciding how elements are laid out on a web page. CSS uses a box model to determine where to place each element -- every element is considered as a rectangular box shape, and those boxes are placed in relation to one another. Each element "box" contains the element content, some space called padding between the content and a border, the border itself, and then surrounding space called a margin. Take a look at some of the following defining properties:

Width and Height: The height and width properties set the height and width of the area where the content of an element box is displayed. This content can be something like the text or image content of an element, or it could include other boxes nested inside. Widths are measured using either pixels (written as 100px, for instance) or by the percentage of the page they cover (a box with a width of 50% would span half the total page width). Heights are measured using pixels and don't use percentages.

You can also set maximum or minimum values for your content boxes instead of defining a size using pixels or percentages. These maximum and minimum values can be set using properties like max-width, max-height, min-width, and min-height. Play around with these attributes to determine which are best for managing the content of your specific web page. Check out the following examples for defining the size of a <div> element:

```
div {
    height: 225px;
    width: 50%;
}
div {
    max-height: 500px;
    min-height: 20px;
    max-width: 300px;
    min-width: 15px;
}
```

Do not set the width or height of your content box to a value that is greater than the size of the browser window in which you are viewing your page. If you do so, the content box will overflow outside of the window and you will need to use the up/down and left/right scroll bars to view the entire box.

Padding: The padding of a content box is the space between the content itself and the edge of the box where a border would be. You can define the padding on each side of your content box individually by using the padding-left, padding-right, padding-top, and padding-bottom properties. Alternatively, you can set the padding for all four sides at once by using the padding property followed by the top, right, bottom, and left padding values. Take a look at each of these methods below for styling a <div> element:

```
div {
    padding-left: 125px;
    padding-right: 20px;
    padding-top: 55px;
    padding-bottom: 110px;
}
div {
    padding: 55px 20px 110px 125px;
}
```

Both of the above rulesets accomplish the same thing. You can also have a padding property that contains 3, 2, or even 1 value instead of 4. If a padding property contains 3 values, the first value corresponds to the padding-top value, the second value corresponds to the padding-right and padding-left values, and the third value corresponds to the padding-bottom value. If a padding property contains 2 values, the first value corresponds to the padding-top and padding-bottom values and the second value corresponds to the padding-left and padding-right values. If a padding property only contains a single value, that value is used for all four sides.

Border: The border for a content box is located between the padding and the margin of the box. The default border size for an element is 0, which would display as nothing, or invisible. However, you can use border-width, border-color, and border-style properties to define a border with a specific thickness, style, and color. You can also use the border, border-left, border-right, border-top, or border-bottom properties to define the style, color, and thickness of a border on one or all sides of your content box. If you'd like to instead set a specific border property on only one side of your content box, you can do that as well by using properties such as border-top-width, border-top-color, or border-top-style. Take a look at some of the ways you might define the styles for the border of a <div> element:

```
div {
    border-left: 2px solid black;
    border-right: 5px solid black;
    border-top: 1px solid red;
    border-bottom: 3px solid red;
}
div {
    border: 2px dashed green;
}


div {
    border-top-style: dotted;
    border-top-color: green;
```

```
    border-top-width: 4px;
    border-bottom-style: double;
    border-bottom-color: purple;
    border-bottom-width: 1px;
    border-left-style: dashed;
    border-left-color: yellow;
    border-left-width: 3px;
    border-right-style: ridge;
    border-right-color: aqua;
    border-right-width: 2px;
}
div {
    border-weight: 2px;
    border-color: blue;
}
```

It is worth noting here that, by default, the background color of an element will extend to the outer edge of the border.

Margin: An element box's margin envelopes the outside margin and demarcates the box from other entities, sort of like an outer padding. You can set the top, right, left, and bottom margins for an element all at once using the margin property, or you can set them individually using the margin-top, margin-bottom, margin-left, and margin-right properties.

The margins from separate elements within a web page can push up against one another and use margin collapsing when they touch. With margin collapsing, the distance between two touching element boxes becomes the larger of the two touching margins instead of the sum of the two touching margins.

Some examples for defining the margins of a <div> element are as follows:

```
div {
    margin: 20px 30px 15px 10px;
```

```
}
div {
    margin-top: 20px;
    margin-right: 30px;
    margin-bottom: 15px;
    margin-left: 10px;
}
```

Similarly to the padding property, the margin property can have anywhere from one to four values. If the margin property has four values, they correspond to the margin's top, right, bottom, and left values, in that order. If the margin property has three values, the first value corresponds to the top margin, the second value corresponds to the left and right margins, and the third value corresponds to the bottom margin. If the margin property has two values, the first value corresponds to the top and bottom margins, and the second value corresponds to the left and right margins. If the margin property only has one value, that value corresponds to all the four margins of the element box.

Using the box model, it is easy to determine to a total actual size that an element will take up on a page. To determine the element's height, add the content box height, the top padding, the bottom padding, the top border, the bottom border, the top margin, and the bottom margin. Similarly, to determine the element's width, add the content box width, the left padding, the right padding, the left border, the right border, the left margin, and the right margin. Note that this method will give you the total space that an element will take up on the web page. If you would instead like to know how big the element will look, perform the same calculations as above without adding in the top margin, the bottom margin, the left margin, or the right margin.

Position: With the position attribute, you can define the location of an element on your page. There are several different values for the position attribute, including static, fixed, relative, absolute, and sticky. These positions are then defined using the top, bottom, right, and left attributes to set the top margin edge, bottom margin edge, right margin edge, or left margin edge location within your page.

The static value is the default for the position attribute, and doesn't really do anything special to the positioning of the element; it will just flow normally with the page:

```
div {
    position: static;
}
```

The fixed value puts an element in a fixed position relative to the viewing port for your web page, and uses the top, bottom, left, and right attributes to define the said position. The following example would place the <div> element into the bottom right corner of your browser window:

```
div {
    position: fixed;
    width: 75px;
    height: 50px;
    right: 0;
    bottom: 0;
}
```

The relative value sets an element's position relative to where it would normally be located on the page and leaves a space in the page where the element would normally be. The following example would move the <div> element over 75 pixels from its default position:

```
div {
    position: relative;
    left: 75px;
}
```

The absolute value allows an element to be positioned in a specific location based on an ancestor's location or the body of the document if no ancestor is present. The following example could be used to position the "little" div in the bottom right corner of the "big" div:

```css
div.big {
    position: relative;
    width: 450px;
    height: 250px;
}
div.little {
    position: absolute;
    bottom: 0;
    right: 0;
    width: 150px;
    height: 75px;
}
```

```html
<!DOCTYPE html>
<html>
   <body>
         <div class="big">
This div is big and has a relative position
<div class="little">
This div is smaller and its position is relative to the big div it is contained in</div>
</div>
</div>
   </body>
</html>
```

The sticky value allows an element to have a position based on a user's scroll position. A sticky element will have a relative position until a user scrolls past it, and then it will "stick" to one position in the viewing window. The following example will cause the <div> element to stay 50 pixels down from the top of the screen once a user scrolls to it:

```css
div {
    position: sticky;
    top: 50px;
}
```

Float: The float property in CSS can be a useful tool when defining your page layouts. One of the most common uses of the float property is to wrap text around images or display images side by side. Or, if you'd like, you can even use the float property to set the layout of your entire web page! The following CSS would cause the <img> elements to float to the right of the text within a paragraph, and allow the text to wrap around the image naturally once it gets long enough:

```
img {
    float: right;
}

<!DOCTYPE html>
<html>
    <body>
            <p><img src="shapes.png">A bunch of text!</p>
    </body>
</html>
```

Clear: The clear property is used along with the float property to further control the layout of a web page. By using the clear property, you can disallow floating elements to the left and right of an element. For instance, the following CSS would make it so that no elements are allowed to float on either side of the <div> element:

```
div {
    clear: both;
}
```

By default, the clear property has a value of none; that is, floating elements are allowed both to the left and to the right of the element.

Let's take a look at some examples of web pages using the properties discussed in this chapter. For the first page, copy and paste or manually type the following HTML into your text editor and save it with a .html extension:

```
<!DOCTYPE html>
<html>
    <head>
        <title>CSS Layout Example</title>
        <link rel="stylesheet" href="styles.css">
    </head>
    <body>
        <div class="news">
            This could tell users about a cool new update for your site!
        </div>
        <div class="pageheader">
            <h1>The header for your webpage!</h1>
        </div>
        <div class="column menu">
            <ul>
                <li>An item in your page menu</li>
                <li>A second item in your page menu</li>
                <li>A third item in your page menu</li>
                <li>A fourth item in your page menu</li>
                <li>A fifth item in your page menu</li>
            </ul>
        </div>
        <div class="column content">
            <h1>This could be a heading for some content on your page</h1>
            <p>This paragraph could welcome users to your website.</p>
            <p>This could be an interesting paragraph about a hobby or an interest that your page is about.</p>
            <p>This could be a followup paragraph for the first.</p>
            <p>This paragraph could give users some instructions on how to navigate your website.</p>
```

```
        </div>
        <div class="pagefooter">
            <p>Here is some text in the footer of your webpage!</p>
        </div>
    </body>
</html>
```

Then, copy and paste or manually type the following CSS into a separate file in your text editor and save it at styles.css:

```
.pageheader, .pagefooter {
    clear: both;
    background-color: black;
    color: white;
    padding: 20px;
}
.column {
    float: left;
}
.menu {
    width: 20%;
    padding: 10px;
}
.content {
    width: 75%;
}

.menu ul {
    list-style-type: none;
    margin: 0;
    padding: 0;
}
.menu li {
    padding: 10px;
    margin-bottom: 10px;
```

```css
    background-color: blue;
    color: aqua;
    text-decoration: bold;
    text-align: center;
}
.news {
    position: sticky;
    background-color: yellow;
    text-align: center;
    top: 20px;
    margin: 0px 5%;
    height: 20px;
    width: 90%;
    border: 2px dashed green;
}
```

Make sure that you saved the HTML file and the CSS file in the same folder, or put the CSS into the <head> element of your HTML document, as in this case:

```html
<!DOCTYPE html>
<html>
    <head>
        <title>CSS Layout Example</title>
        <style>
.pageheader, .pagefooter {
    clear: both;
    background-color: black;
    color: white;
    padding: 20px;
}
.column {
    float: left;
}
.menu {
    width: 20%;
```

```css
    padding: 10px;
}
.content {
    width: 75%;
}
.menu ul {
    list-style-type: none;
    margin: 0;
    padding: 0;
}
.menu li {
    padding: 10px;
    margin-bottom: 10px;
    background-color: blue;
    color: aqua;
    text-decoration: bold;
    text-align: center;
}
.news {
    position: sticky;
    background-color: yellow;
    text-align: center;
    top: 20px;
    margin: 0px 5%;
    height: 20px;
    width: 90%;
    border: 2px dashed green;
}
        </style>
    </head>
    <body>

            <div class="news">
                This could tell users about a cool new update for your site!
```

```html
        </div>

        <div class="pageheader">
            <h1>The header for your webpage!</h1>
        </div>

        <div class="column menu">
            <ul>
                <li>An item in your page menu</li>
                <li>A second item in your page menu</li>
                <li>A third item in your page menu</li>
                <li>A fourth item in your page menu</li>
                <li>A fifth item in your page menu</li>
            </ul>
        </div>

        <div class="column content">
            <h1>This could be a heading for some content on your page</h1>
            <p>This paragraph could welcome users to your website.</p>
            <p>This could be an interesting paragraph about a hobby or an interest that your page is about.</p>
            <p>This could be a followup paragraph for the first.</p>
            <p>This paragraph could give users some instructions on how to navigate your website.</p>
        </div>

        <div class="pagefooter">
            <p>Here is some text in the footer of your webpage!</p>
        </div>
    </body>
```

</html>

Then, open the HTML file with your browser. The resulting page should look similar to this:

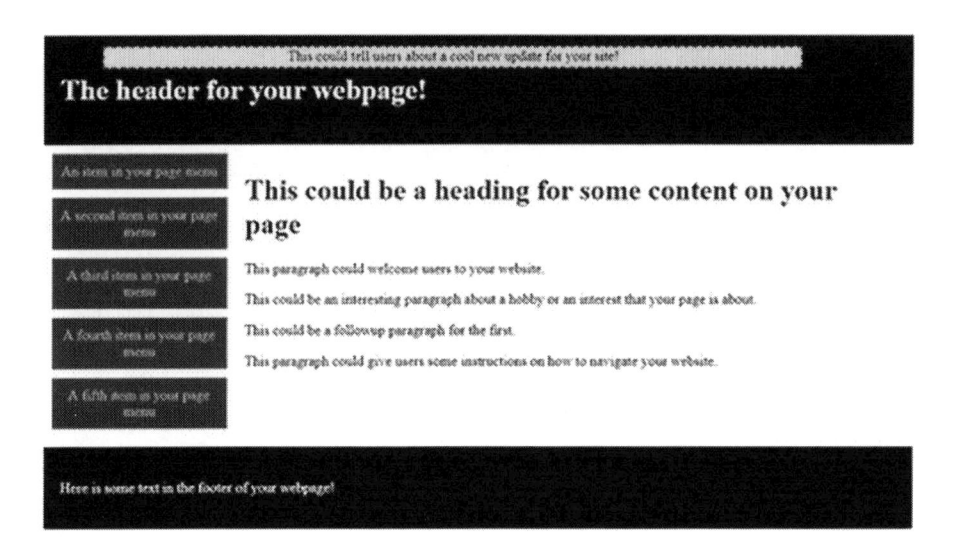

For this next example, copy and paste or manually type the following HTML into your text editor and save it with an .html extension:

```
<!DOCTYPE html>
<html>
   <head>
      <title>CSS Layout Example</title>
      <link rel="stylesheet" href="styles.css">
   </head>
   <body>

      <div class="pagealert">
         This box will always show at the bottom of the page. Use it for news or alerts!
      </div>

      <div class="pageheader">
```

```html
        <h1>Put some text here to display in your page header!</h1>
    </div>

    <ul>
        <li><a class="active" href="#home">A menu item</a></li>
        <li><a href="#page1">A second menu item</a></li>
        <li><a href="#page2">A third menu item</a></li>
        <li><a href="#page3">A fourth menu item</a></li>
    </ul>

    <div class="content">
        <h1>This could be a heading for some content on your page</h1>
        <p>This paragraph could welcome users to your website.</p>
        <p>This could be an interesting paragraph about a hobby or an interest that your page is about.</p>
        <p>This could be a followup paragraph for the first.</p>
        <p>This paragraph could give users some instructions on how to navigate your website.</p>
    </div>

            <img class="galleryitem" src="shapes.png">
            <img class="galleryitem" src="rectangle.png">
            <img class="galleryitem" src="triangle.png">
            <img class="galleryitem" src="oval.png">
            <img class="galleryitem" src="shapes.png">
            <img class="galleryitem" src="rectangle.png">
            <img class="galleryitem" src="triangle.png">
```

```
            <img class="galleryitem" src="oval.png">
            <img class="galleryitem" src="shapes.png">
            <img class="galleryitem" src="rectangle.png">
            <img class="galleryitem" src="triangle.png">
            <img class="galleryitem" src="oval.png">
            <img class="galleryitem" src="shapes.png">
            <img class="galleryitem" src="rectangle.png">
            <img class="galleryitem" src="triangle.png">
            <img class="galleryitem" src="oval.png">

            <div class="content">
                <p>This paragraph could contain descriptions about the photos in your gallery.</p>
            </div>

            <div class="pagefooter">
                <p>Here is some text in the footer of your webpage!</p>
            </div>
     </body>
</html>
```

Then, copy and paste or manually type the following CSS into a separate file in your text editor and save it at styles.css:

```
.pageheader, .pagefooter {
    clear: both;
    background-color: grey;
    color: aqua;
    font-family: arial;
    padding: 15px;
}
.pageheader {
    font-size: 28px;
```

```css
}
.pagefooter {
  margin-bottom: 50px;
  text-align: center;
}
.galleryitem {
  float: left;
  width: 31%;
  margin: 1%;
  border: 1px solid green;
}
.content {
  float: left;
  width: 100%;
}
ul {
  list-style-type: none;
  margin: 0;
  padding: 0;
  overflow: hidden;
  background-color: #333;
}
li {
  float: left;
}
li a {
  display: inline-block;
  color: white;
  text-align: center;
  padding: 14px 16px;
  text-decoration: none;
}
li a:hover {
  background-color: orange;
}
```

```css
.active {
   background-color: black;
}
.pagealert {
   position: fixed;
   background-color: red;
   text-align: center;
   text-decoration: bold;
   color: white;
   bottom: 20px;
   margin: 0px 25%;
   width: 50%;
   border: 3px double black;
}
```

Make sure that you saved the HTML file and the CSS file in the same folder, or just include the CSS in the HTML <head> element, like so:

```html
<!DOCTYPE html>
<html>
   <head>
      <title>CSS Layout Example</title>
      <style>
.pageheader, .pagefooter {
   clear: both;
   background-color: grey;
   color: aqua;
   font-family: arial;
   padding: 15px;
}
.pageheader {
   font-size: 28px;
}
.pagefooter {
   margin-bottom: 50px;
   text-align: center;
```

```css
}
.galleryitem {
    float: left;
    width: 31%;
    margin: 1%;
    border: 1px solid green;
}
.content {
    float: left;
    width: 100%;
}
ul {
    list-style-type: none;
    margin: 0;
    padding: 0;
    overflow: hidden;
    background-color: #333;
}
li {
    float: left;
}
li a {
    display: inlinc-block;
    color: white;
    text-align: center;
    padding: 14px 16px;
    text-decoration: none;
}
li a:hover {
    background-color: orange;
}
.active {
    background-color: black;
}
.pagealert {
```

```
    position: fixed;
    background-color: red;
    text-align: center;
    text-decoration: bold;
    color: white;
    bottom: 20px;
    margin: 0px 25%;
    width: 50%;
    border: 3px double black;
}
    </style>
</head>
<body>

    <div class="pagealert">
        This box will always show at the bottom of the page. Use it for news or alerts!
    </div>

    <div class="pageheader">
        <h1>Put some text here to display in your page header!</h1>
    </div>

    <ul>
        <li><a class="active" href="#home">A menu item</a></li>
        <li><a href="#page1">A second menu item</a></li>
        <li><a href="#page2">A third menu item</a></li>
        <li><a href="#page3">A fourth menu item</a></li>
    </ul>
```

```html
<div class="content">
    <h1>This could be a heading for some content on your page</h1>
    <p>This paragraph could welcome users to your website.</p>
    <p>This could be an interesting paragraph about a hobby or an interest that your page is about.</p>
    <p>This could be a followup paragraph for the first.</p>
    <p>This paragraph could give users some instructions on how to navigate your website.</p>
</div>

<img class="galleryitem" src="shapes.png">
<img class="galleryitem" src="rectangle.png">
<img class="galleryitem" src="triangle.png">
<img class="galleryitem" src="oval.png">
<img class="galleryitem" src="shapes.png">
<img class="galleryitem" src="rectangle.png">
<img class="galleryitem" src="triangle.png">
<img class="galleryitem" src="oval.png">
<img class="galleryitem" src="shapes.png">
<img class="galleryitem" src="rectangle.png">
<img class="galleryitem" src="triangle.png">
<img class="galleryitem" src="oval.png">
<img class="galleryitem" src="shapes.png">
<img class="galleryitem" src="rectangle.png">
<img class="galleryitem" src="triangle.png">
<img class="galleryitem" src="oval.png">

<div class="content">
    <p>This paragraph could contain descriptions about the photos in your gallery.</p>
</div>
```

```
        <div class="pagefooter">
            <p>Here is some text in the footer of your webpage!</p>
        </div>
    </body>
</html>
```

Now, open the HTML file with your browser. The resulting page should look similar to this:

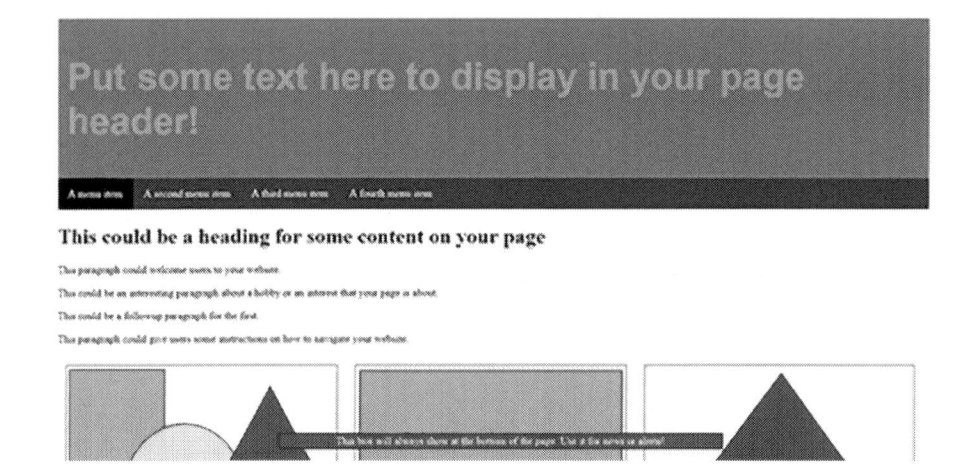

Once you have this page opened in your browser, see what happens if you scroll down the page or resize the browser window. For some practice, see if you can create a .css file that contains elements that retain their size when the window is made smaller or larger.

Chapter 4

Polishing Your Web Pages With CSS

In order to ensure that your web pages are displaying properly, it's important to frequently check your HTML and CSS files and debug them when necessary. Both HTML and CSS are permissive, so you don't have to worry about "breaking" you web page if you make a mistake. Even, if you use an invalid CSS declaration or an unsupported feature your browser will simply ignore the error and proceed to the next declaration. This can often be beneficial since a single error won't bring down your entire page -- the browser just won't display your content as expected. However, it can sometimes be difficult to figure out how to fix an improperly displayed element if you aren't sure what is causing the discrepancy. Fortunately, there are a couple of different ways to handle this issue.

The first way to try and debug a problematic web page is by using your browser's page inspector tool and CSS editor. To open up the page inspector tool, simply right click within a web page. In this example, we'll be using a Chrome browser to inspect one of the web pages you created in the previous chapter. If you aren't using Chrome, that's okay! Other browsers will offer you the same features, although they might be accessed in a slightly different way. With Chrome, once you right click within a web page, you simply need to choose "Inspect" from the pop up menu to open the page inspector tool. It will look something like this:

You can also use Ctrl + Shift + I to open the inspect panel in Google Chrome.

Now, take a look at the panel that has opened up. In the top portion, you can view the HTML that is used to display the page. In the lower right portion, you can view a graphical representation of each element's size, padding, border, and margin. In the lower left portion, you can see a block with tabs labeled Styles, Event Listeners, DOM Breakpoints, and Properties. We'll be working in the tab labeled Styles for this example.

To use the CSS Editor tool, first, click on an element in the top portion of the Inspect panel (where the HTML is displayed). For instance, let's click on the line that says <div class="news">. When you do so, you should see the contents of the Style tab below change to reflect the CSS that is used when displaying that element. If a CSS declaration is invalid for any reason, it will appear with a line through it in this window, along with a warning symbol. Also, if you hover over the attributes in this window, you will notice that they each have a checkbox to their left. You can click this checkbox to toggle the CSS attribute in the page.

Try this out now. Click the checkbox next to the text-align attribute and notice how this affects the way the news alert box displays on your web page on the left of the screen. The property will have a line through it when you click the checkbox to toggle it off. If you click on the value to the right of the properties in the Style tab, you are given the option to enter a new value. You can also click on the colored boxes next to properties with a color value to change the color and instantly view how your page will be affected.

You can probably already understand how this can be a useful tool when trying to find and fix errors in your CSS. Not only can you instantly view any invalid CSS, you can easily manipulate the values for each of the properties of any element. By this, you can see how they affect how that element is displayed. You can easily view all of the CSS that is associated with an element. This is especially beneficial when working with elements that use multiple classes. You can even choose to temporarily ignore a certain property to check whether or not that is causing your page to display incorrectly. With these tools, you have a huge advantage in finding errors within your CSS over simply reading through your .css file manually!

If you'd rather not use the Page Inspector and CSS Editor in your browser, another option for finding errors in your CSS is to use a CSS Validator. You can find a CSS Validator online with a simple Google search. The validator should allow you to upload your CSS file, link to a web page online, or manually type some CSS into a text area. Then, the validator will comb through your CSS and display any errors it encounters along with the line numbers where they are located and the selectors that are associated with them. For instance, your CSS validator tool might tell you that there is an error in your .news class on line 35 that has occurred due to a missing semicolon or a misspelled property name.

Although using a CSS validator tool can be beneficial in some circumstances, there are many times it won't be able to provide you with the information you need to fix your display issues. For instance, if your page is displaying incorrectly because you typed the wrong value into your CSS file, the validator won't display an error since the syntax of the declaration is technically correct. Similarly, if you use the wrong selector when defining the styles for your page, the validator won't catch the error since nothing is syntactically incorrect. The best use of a CSS validator is probably as a precursor to using the Page Inspector method above -- the CSS validator will catch any basic errors in the syntax of your CSS, and you'll be able to fix them before addressing selector, property, and value issues with the built in browser CSS editor.

Try running a few of the examples from this book through a CSS validator and then view them with your browser's Inspect feature to familiarize yourself with both methods. That's it! Now you're ready to create, view, and debug your own HTML and CSS projects.

Chapter 5

CSS Animations

One of the cool and more recent things to come into CSS is the concept of CSS animations. CSS animations are great because they allow your site to be fluid and allow you to, as it sounds, animate your HTML code.

In the past, animating your code was pretty tedious. It was something you had to do through a combination of JavaScript code and clever CSS/HTML scripting. That or, in even older days, you'd have to animate your site through the use of Flash. This led to sites being extremely clunky, hard to interact with, tacky, and altogether much lower quality than they are today.

That all changed with the advent of CSS3. CSS3 now allows you to subtly animate your site in various ways that weren't available to programmers before. This is great because it means that there's an even greater chance that your site can be run without cumbersome scripts or anything of that nature.

The first part of CSS animations rests in keyframes. Keyframes allow you to set important events that happen throughout the course of an animation. You can name your keyframes and then refer to those at a later point. Let's say, for example, that we wanted to shift the text color from black to aqua. We could do this like so:

```
@keyframes myText {
    from {color: black;}
    to {color:yellow;}
}
```

You could then refer to this at a later point using *myText* as the animation name. You can give a certain animation description to an element by defining the animation name and then defining the length of the duration.

Note also that you can actually instead of using *from* and *to*, define the *percentages* at which these keyframes will take place. 0% describes the starting state, 100% describes the ending state, and anything between will ensure that the element takes on that property at that point within the overall duration of the animation.

Let's say we had an element called *myDiv* that we wanted to use our previous animation with:

```
#myDiv {
    animation-name: myText;
    animation-duration: 2s;
}
```

You can take this a step further by using CSS selectors. CSS selectors allow you to change the state of a given element when a certain event happens. Let's say, for example, that you wanted to specify an animation to happen exclusively when you hovered over a certain div. You could do so using the *hover* selector. Then, within the element description for the hover selector, you would put the animation data.

```
#myDiv {
    // raw data goes here
}
#myDiv:hover {
    animation-name: myText;
    animation-duration:2s;
}
```

This would cause the on-load data from the initial definition to happen when the page is loaded. The style of the element would change whenever the element was hovered over, thanks to the hover selector.

Therefore, whenever the element with the ID "myDiv" was hovered over, the specified animation would take place. Make sense? It's pretty simple!

There are a number of different CSS selectors that you can use.

hover will become active whenever the element is hovered over.

active is used in reference to anchor links and refers to the page that you're actively on. *a:active* will select any links on the page that link back to the page you are currently on and then style them in the way that you specify.

::after will insert data after the content of any given specified element.

::before will insert data before the content of any given specified element.

There are many more, but these are the most common ones and are therefore the ones that you are most likely going to be seeing often. Hover especially is the one that you'll most likely make the most use of.

With that, we've covered the basics of CSS animations. In the following chapter, we're going to be talking about how you can actually implement everything we've covered so far in this book in a few more modern web design paradigms. Stay tuned!

Chapter 6

Trends in CSS - Fixed Width Sites

One of the older trends in website design is actually essential to cover because it will give you a prime basis and starting point for the rest of your website design. One thing that we haven't really talked about at this point is actually culminating everything that you've worked with into a cohesive design, so we're going to be doing that in this chapter as we try to shamble together a lot of the concepts that we've covered into one bigger vision.

Web design is all about presentation. It's important that in your design path, you choose a way which presents your end vision in a way that makes it appealing to anybody who might come across your site. The most immediate way to get practice with this - and, indeed, the easiest - is to start with the most simple form of higher-level website design in CSS that is still applicable in today's web design market.

While you aren't going to come across many sites from established designers that utilize fixed-width constructions these days, it's still important that you understand the methodology and the thought process because it will actually teach you quite a bit about design in the process.

Fixed width designs have their basis in the fact that when you design a website, you want its presentation to be uniform. You want what the users see to be what you see. This can be difficult when you're dealing with all of the different computers and display resolutions out there. The way that early web designers would deal with this problem was by designing sites in such a way that anybody with any computer would see the same exact thing, provided that their viewport was beyond a certain width.

As at the time of writing this book, there really aren't many computers out there running on hardware updated enough to use a modern web browser that will have a smaller resolution than 1280x1024 - even mobile devices normally have a greater width than 960. If you go really old, such as iPhone second generation and prior, you'll run into widths that are in the 400s, but there's running on 10-year-old technology and very, very old mobile phones. So, you can trust that most people who would be accessing your site in the current climate would have a width greater than 960.

Most resolutions for computers generally have a width of at least 1366, with most desktop computers having a resolution width of at least 1920.

So what does this mean? This means that by finding a resolution that all of these devices can display and then show everything within that width, you assure that any device that has a resolution of that size or greater can display the content of your website in a seamless and uniform manner.

You've almost certainly in your time on the internet come across sites that do this in a pretty subtle way. One of the more popular web design magazines/periodicals, for example, uses this format in such a way that a given user would find it difficult to tell that this was the design principle. Because of the subtlety, regularity, and simplicity, this is a great place for future would-be web designers to start off.

So how does this work? The main philosophy of fixed-width design is having everything on your site fit within a certain container. This container sits on top of your background but contains all of your content. It will normally have a certain width affixed to it. A width of 900 or 1000 pixels is considered both standard and safe. Your code may end up looking like this:

```
<!DOCTYPE html>
```

```html
<html>
    <head>
        <title>My site</title>
        <style>
            html, body, background {
                margin:0px;
                padding:0px;
                background:#d0d0d0;
            }
            #container {
                width:900px;
                margin-left:auto;
                margin-right:auto;
                border-left:1px solid #efefef;
                border-right:1px solid #efefef;
            }
        </style>
    </head>
    <body>
        <div id="container">
            Container example.
        </div>
    </body>
</html>
```

The automatic left and right margins would center the div element. Your content would then fit pretty safely within this container. Your content could go in here and you could scale your content according to these widths. This means you could use exact pixel numbers and ensure that the design would actually look the same regardless of the platform that it was being viewed on. This is of the utmost importance in terms of overall usability and presentation and was, in fact, one of the main draws in using a fixed width design.

There are numerous drawbacks to using a fixed width design, though. The first of them is that it simply doesn't look as good as certain other kinds of designs do. For example, using exact widths means necessarily that your design won't be able to scale up to the beautiful and breathtaking artistic designs of the responsive designs that we'll be discussing in the next chapter.

This can be a massive drawback because as a web designer, you want your end result to look pretty. You want it to be flashy, effective, and showcase your abilities as well as the key point that the site is trying to convey. You want to show what you're able to do because web design is an artistic medium like any other form of design.

However, there are many cases where the simpler design and faster turnaround time and more exact and simplistic nature can be preferable. For example, many industrial designs will prefer, to one extent or another, the fixed-width design because it's less distracting and flashy. It lets people just do what they need to do with minimal intervention on the design side. It is an effective and simple design which gets out of the way and works even on older browsers and legacy systems.

Chapter 7

Trends In CSS - Responsive Design

The point of this book is to get you up to speed with CSS and feeling like you understand what you're doing. The hope is that by the end, you'll feel confident enough with the essential information pertaining to CSS and related disciplines that you'll be able to start designing your own sites.

One of the key parts of this is that we cover what could be considered the primary trends in CSS and web design at the moment. These are the most common as at the time of writing this book, but it does exclude certain frameworks which one could consider to be beyond the scope of this book, like React.JS or things similar in nature.

The first thing that we're going to talk about is *responsive web design*. Responsive web design arose in reaction to the trend of smartphone market dominance in web design. More and more people are having access to smartphones. They also have access to instantaneous web access regardless of where they were. Consequently, it began to become necessary to create intricate mobile designs which went beyond the low-data mobile versions of yesteryear from the eras of Blackberries and Palm Pres. In the face of high resolution mobile browsers and smartphones such as the iPhone and Samsung Galaxy, it was necessary to have a way for web design. This way, it could mimic the strengths of these mobile browsers and remove the need for a separate mobile version of the site. In the alternative, we are opting for a version of the site relative to the screen resolution of the device being used.

While this hasn't completely invalidated the mobile versions of sites, it does create a sort of situation where one can address them in a different way. Before, mobile sites were addressed by a JavaScript or HTML preprocessor directive that would cause the page to redirect if a certain browser was detected. With the advent of CSS3, it became possible to detect screen resolutions and automatically adjust the site in response rather than having a site being entirely readjusted.

Part of responsive design involves having designs that are artistically and aesthetically pleasing rather than just being fully functional. In this capacity, responsive designs serve as a means to make designs more expressive on the designer's end and more interactive and intuitive on the user's end.

So, what is responsive design? You've more than likely see the the responsive design before. If you've run into a web page that takes up the entire width and height of your browser window and that scales appropriately regardless of how large your browser window is at any given moment.

The way that responsive design works can take many different forms but the essence of responsive design comes down to essentially just everything being efficiently and easily scalable. It also should respond to the size of the viewport, or the overall viewing resolution of the browser. You can test out different viewport sizes in a responsive design by actually sizing your browser up and down both vertically and horizontally using your operating system's built-in sizing mechanisms.

Responsive designs work on the basis of things scaling with width and height values. You can accomplish this by using percentage-based sizing in your document. This is the basic idea, anyhow; the rest of it - which is a little bit beyond the scope of a beginner book - is actually using CSS commands in order to change the style of the document if, for example, the viewport were less than a certain width or height. For right now, we're just going to focus on how to implement scaling heights and widths.

The first thing you need to bear in mind is that when you test this out by scaling your window size up and down, you will notice that the size of the divisions will actually grow larger and smaller. This is perfect! It is exactly what is meant to happen.

The first thing that you need to realize about CSS width and height properties is that they inherit from the element larger than them. So, for example, you can't just say that divs of a certain class will have a height of, say, 20%. There is no definition of what 20% is even *of*. 20% of... what, exactly? In order for this statement to have any sort of meaning behind it, you need to realize that 20% is supposed to be a percentage of something else. If you say 20%, then this statement is somewhat inherently meaningless unless you indicate the 20% is a percentage of.

The way that you do this is by defining some parent object with a percentage. The greatest parent object is the *body* element, so any elements located within the *body* element can only be based on the *percentage* that is defined for the *body* element. Make sense? So if you want something to be 20%, then the body element has to have a parent height that this can be based on.

The body element will automatically use percentage based heights as a function of the viewport's size. However, if you were to define the body height as something like 1000 pixels, and had a div that was 20% height, then the div would base its 20% of the nearest parent element - here, body - and therefore have a height of 200 pixels.

Let's look at this a little bit more in-depth. The first thing you would have to do for scaling heights and widths is defined your body height as the height of the viewport. This will let everything else be a function of that when you define their heights and widths with percentages. In order to define your body as the height and width of the viewport, you're going to want to put the following in your code:

```
html, body, background {
    height:100%;
```

```
    width:100%;
}
```

Every div that you define afterward that has the body element as its most immediate parent element (as in, it isn't nested within another div element) will scale based on this. So, if you were to make a div now that was set to have a height of, say, 50%, it would take up 50% of the screen height.

In modern web design, this really comes to present itself in two different ways. The first is through the development of one-page designs, and the other way is through the development of grid-based design layouts. We'll spend a brief moment going over both of these so you have an idea of how they work.

One-page designs essentially are divided into sections. They'll usually have a splash opener to the site that talks about the site and its primary purpose, as well as a navigational bar or button you can click in order to open a navigational panel. Both of these will move with the page as you scroll down.

Now, you can start to move down the web page. Generally, all of the sections are the size of one viewport. There are often some neat transitions added in or other things that will cause the scrolling between sections to feel easy or even seamless. Others, still, will use parallax scrolling techniques in order to make the background stay exactly where it is as the user scrolls down the page.

Let's talk for a second about parallax scrolling before we move on to the next section of this chapter. Parallax scrolling is relatively intuitive and also pretty beautiful in its own right when done correctly. It's a snazzy feature that can be seriously cool when implemented well.

Parallax scrolling is essentially when the background moves in some way in response to the user scrolling. This runs counter to the standard wherein the background image or background of a given section doesn't necessarily stay with the user as they scroll. This might sound difficult, but it's actually rather simple.

You can implement parallax scrolling by setting a background image for the given section and then fix its position:

background-position: fixed;

This will lead the background position to scroll with the user as they move up and down the page. Interspersed with clever design, this can be an absolutely killer way to showcase your design abilities while not roughing up your code or making it excessively difficult. Bare this in mind, because this is a massive trend in web design these days and you're going to be seeing it a lot.

Through other CSS features and JavaScript events, you can add even more things to implement within your code base which will make your design more appealing or more intuitive. The combination of HTML5, CSS3, and JavaScript is extremely powerful. Some people have even created full-on games in just these 3 languages. So, it's important that you have a grasp on them and how they work because by doing so, you're setting yourself up for success in terms of long-term design potential.

The other way that these responsive designs tend to be implemented is through the use of grid-based layouts. Grid-based layouts are becoming more and more common as time presses on. Their particular handiness comes from the fact that, first and foremost, they offer a very convenient modular method of development. Moreover, they allow you to design a simple and beautiful site using pre-developed and prefixed dimensions. This makes your entire development process far easier.

An example of a grid-based layout would be something which, for example, uses a 3 wide grid where 3 elements are fit into one row. In addition, these rows are roughly 30% width each, perhaps with a 3% margin on either side and a 2% margin in between. This would allow the information to be presented in a clean and pragmatic manner.

The grid-based layout is one of the other very popular methods of design because it allows for the combination of multiple different manners of layouts within the context of a grid-based system.

Grid-based designs fill, to some degree, the industrial void that fixed-width sites used to fill. While fixed-width sites do still exist, when simple and effective designs that look modern are needed, they are usually accomplished using some form of grid-based design. This also is an ideal choice for online store fronts because it's unpretentious and rather easy to use.

With that, we've covered the other monolith of modern web design: the responsive website. As I said, there's quite a bit more to it than all of this, but it's something that you're mainly going to get experience and exposure to through practice.

Conclusion

Thank you again for purchasing *CSS: Basic Fundamental Guide For Beginners*, and congratulations on making it to the end! Hopefully, you've gained some insight into how to use CSS selectors, discovered how to effectively create layouts for your web pages, and had some fun exploring the different ways CSS can enhance your websites.

The next step is to let yourself be creative. Have an idea for a unique new web page? Try to apply the techniques you learned throughout this book to make it a reality! Practice makes perfect, just like with any other skill, so be sure to put in the time to polish your techniques. There are countless new websites out there just waiting for someone to create them, and that means countless opportunities for you to hone your skills.

Finally, if you found this book useful as you began on your CSS journey, please take a moment to review it on Amazon. Thank you, good luck, and enjoy your new and improved websites!

JavaScript

Basic Fundamental Guide for Beginners

Introduction

Congratulations on purchasing *JavaScript : Basic Fundamental Guide for Beginners* and thank you for doing so.

The following chapters will discuss how to program using JavaScript. We're going to start from the very beginning and explain program logic as we make our way through this broad topic and try to uncover everything as possible.

JavaScript is immensely popular. Therefore, you're doing the right thing by trying to learn it. My goal is to give you all of the tools and information you need to become a fantastic JavaScript programmer in no time at all.

There are plenty of books on this subject on the market. Thanks again for choosing this one! Every effort was made to ensure that this book is packed with useful information. Please enjoy!

Chapter 1

History of JavaScript

This book is going to tackle a couple of hefty questions and also assume that you've got little to no practical programming experience. The reason for this is that, for a lot of people, JavaScript is their first language. Many people start out with something like web development or perhaps with a recommendation from a friend and find that JavaScript is one of the "easiest" languages to learn.

This is a bit of a misnomer of course; I've helped a lot of people learn to program. Some benefit more from a language that is more abstract and easier to understand, such as JavaScript. Others still benefit more from languages where everything is a concept and put right in front of them to toy with, because the verbosity helps them to understand what they're working within a better sense, such as Java or C++.

Regardless of these, I'm going to assume, since you're here, that you're in the first camp, as well as explain things with enough rigor so that you'll still understand the language well if you're already in the second camp. JavaScript is not a difficult first language. Actually, it's far from it. It's easy to understand, abstract, and master. However, there is a definite degree of challenge that comes with, such as getting out of your comfort zone and learning all of the little concepts related to programming itself.

Therefore, let's think for a second. What is JavaScript? JavaScript is a programming language. A programming language is basically something that allows you to talk to computers and instruct them on what to do. We know for a fact that computers don't understand English. In fact, they don't even understand programming languages. When you break it down, you'll find that computers only really understand things in terms of binary codes - a sequence of ones and zeroes. This is where the name of the computer comes from a *computer*.

The computer makes millions of tiny computations that you can't see every single second. All of these computations are performed using these ones and zeroes that are present at the very smallest level of the computer that you can't see. Knowing this, we've figured out over the years that these ones and zeroes could be controlled and manipulated, first, through the development of languages that work with the processor of the computer itself (assembly) and, second, through the development of languages that serve as the connection between the complex zeroes and ones and the programmer.

As computers have gotten more popular and stronger these days, people who are interested in programming want to learn languages that aren't absurdly difficult to use and understand. As a result, over time, programming languages too have become much simpler as more people started programming as a hobby. The increased processing power of computers over the years and the standardization of an object-oriented paradigm have led to the development of far simpler languages.

In order to understand JavaScript itself, we have to first learn it's history. In the 1970s, there was a place called Bell Labs, a research lab owned and managed by AT&T. A lot of important technological advances originated from Bell Labs. One of the most important ones that you've probably heard before is the *Unix* system.

Unix was a landmark. It was an open-source and simple operating system that was intuitive enough that it could easily be marketed to businesses, developers, and universities all in tandem with one another without encroaching on each other's markets. This was spurred by the development of the C programming language.

The C programming language itself has it's long line of history, but essentially it was the first simple and intuitive language that almost anybody can figure out. It offers a layer of abstraction from the system itself and also offers the programmer the ability to scrutinize the system buildup and therefore understand the computer much better. This allows the programmer to directly manage things, such as memory allocation, or the amount of memory being used by the program in order to perform certain processes. In short, C allows programmers to better understand the system. However, they are expected to handle a great amount of difficult information and are prone to manipulate, for example, the computer's processing capabilities.

Unix would eventually be rewritten in C instead of the standard Assembly code. This is part of the reason why C became so famous. This was a huge deal because it means that any processor that can run a C compiler, that is, the program which converts human-readable programming code to Assembly code that the computer can understand can run Unix as well. Now, this program can be compiled in any system that has a C compiler. This made the program extremely popular worldwide.

Moreover, since C is open source, universities often teach their students the language so that even if they cannot immediately compile Unix for their computers, they can at least modify the code so that they *can* run Unix on them. In addition, Unix is beneficial to C and vice versa because, first, C is being taught in universities to allow students to gain experience first before handling their Unix courses and, second, because Unix comes with a C compiler which makes it even easier for people to write and run codes on Unix systems.

This may seem like an irrelevant detail, but it's a pretty important factor in the overall development of JavaScript and is a key part in the development of modern programming languages in general. This is because these languages can inspire a ton of different languages. For example, the extremely popular languages Java, Python, and C++ all have been – to one extent or another – inspired by C.

JavaScript is no exception. However, with that context, let's think back what the computing landscape was like in the late 80s and early 90s. The general population was slowly being introduced with computers because of the popularity of both C and Unix. The combined popularity and accessibility of these mean that a lot of applications are being built for a lot of computers, approximately exponentially more every year.

However, the Internet was still in its infancy in many ways. Web browsers, for example, were unpopular and nowhere near their technological peak. Web browsers were, in many ways, much more simple and unsophisticated as were web pages themselves.

Currently, web pages primarily consist of just basic text markup rendered through HTML. This book isn't going to tackle HTML except when it's necessary. Therefore, a working knowledge about it is assumed. JavaScript is, after all, one of the three core web development languages alongside HTML and CSS. So, it's worthwhile to learn HTML and CSS as well.

Anyhow, early web browsers were known as *static web pages*. Static web pages are the opposite of *dynamic* web pages, which are web pages that are designed to reflect and render text and images only. Basically, once a static web page is loaded, it cannot be changed from within the page without changing and the reloading the *web file*.

Dynamic web pages – or pages that can be changed in real-time without altering the web file itself – are implemented through what is called *client-side scripting*. Client-side scripting is about allowing changes to happen on a web page exclusively on the browser side. That is, client-side scripting allows sophisticated logic and dynamic changes to run within the context of the user's web browser. Any changes are made their machine and within their browser and don't necessarily indicate the transfer of information to a server.

Essentially, JavaScript and all related languages are about giving life to web pages. It's about taking web pages and making them able to do things instead of just be still. This functionality was, for a long time, just a glimmer in the eye of people who were looking forward to web development. However, this doesn't mean that scripting didn't exist way before. There was early support for technologies designed to allow web pages to interact more. However, these were very rudimentary. The early graphical web browsers were capable of scripting even during its infancy.

This resulted in the creation of another browser, *Mozilla* which inspired the development of Firefox. Currently, however, Firefox was far from being a factor. Officially, the browser was released as *Netscape*, which was known by many as being among the most popular browsers in the 90s, and if you used a computer in the 90s, then you probably were using Netscape.

In the mid-90s, the idea of embedded codes in web pages – that is, codes written in other programming languages that can be inserted directly into and run from a web page – started becoming even more popular. However, there still wasn't enough information regarding the process of practical embedded languages. Java did somewhat serve the purpose, but it wasn't simple. In fact, it died out because it entails a great amount of raw computing power for it to be used. A better alternative was needed, something that can be directly embedded into and alter the web page. Such a thing didn't exist.

Netscape decided to create a scripting language that can run within HTML documents and be easily embedded and interpreted within the browser itself. The language was supposed to display a similar syntax to Java and C++. This was to differentiate it from other popular scripting languages at that time, such as Perl, Python, and Lisp. Believe it or not, a C-inspired scripting language was relatively nouveau at the time.

The language was first released as LiveScript and then later was changed to *JavaScript*. JavaScript became the final name of the language from that on, most likely as an attempt by Netscape to capitalize the success of the Java programming language that was extremely popular at the time, even though JavaScript wasn't particularly related to Java except in its syntactic in some places.

JavaScript was initially only implemented for client-side scripting or the creation of dynamic web pages (as we've already discussed). The first server-side implementation of JavaScript appeared a year or so after the initial release of JavaScript. Today, the server-side JavaScript is still being implemented even though its implementations are far less common than those of the client-side.

The mid-90s showed the development of many now-important web technologies and also browser wars. JavaScript plays an important part in the browser wars, which gained popularity pretty quickly and was implemented by Netscape in their browser. However, Netscape's primary opponent during that time, Internet Explorer, didn't have a support for JavaScript.

This started to change in late 1996. It was clear that some kind of business-wide standard for JavaScript was needed in order for the World Wide Web to be accessed by all browsers. In order to do this, Netscape sent their language into a standards board in order for the language to be reviewed and standardized. The language standard was called ECMAScript, which was published in 1997. This standardization became the starting point for many different languages and is a language in its own right. It's the *standard* of a language, upon which other languages are derived from. All of these different derivations are referred to as *implementations* of the standard. JavaScript is the most popular one, but there were a few others that transpired, such as ActionScript designed for Flash coding.

With the standardization of ECMAScript, JavaScript was finally being used by other browsers and not just Netscape. JavaScript was an ambition in the mid-2000s. During this time, JavaScript and the things for which it could be used were becoming popular to the public (especially the developers) after the development of a white paper wherein Ajax was defined, basically promising the development of extremely dynamic web pages as opposed to the static pages prior. This resulted in the development of many more technologies that can be used alongside JavaScript, such as jQuery, which remained until 2015 or 2016.

A little later in the Oughts, there was at last cohesive work done in order to push the status of the JavaScript language forward and force new standards fit for new technologies. Since then, newer implementations and constant unified updates have been created to develop a unified version of ECMAScript. Therefore, all implementations of ECMA, including JavaScript, resulted in the development of more technical possibilities.

For the last few years, new standards of ECMAScript have been released every year.

The major breakthrough of JavaScript must have been Ajax when developers began to take interest and supported the language. Today, there is an even greater need for an extensive browser support, and JavaScript began to push for that spotlight. Since then, it has become the most widely used web scripting language.

The history of JavaScript shows that it has undergone challenges to become what it is today. I hope that you appreciated the path that it has taken. In the following chapter, we're going to discuss exactly where we *are* at today and all of the different things that JavaScript can be used for.

Chapter 2

How JavaScript is Used

Currently, JavaScript is used for a number of different uses in the mainstream web framework. It is implemented through a number of different layers like *React.js* or *Bootstrap.js*.

Raw JavaScript is fairly uncommon today and is used only to build bigger projects and APIs. Many of these are open source, and you will encounter raw JavaScript generally whenever you're working with these open source projects and not so often in your raw code.

For a long time – though not so often now – jQuery was one of the most popular JavaScript libraries, if not the most popular. You can still sometimes find it lingering around, but it has largely been outpaced by other more popular web frameworks.

This introduces the most popular use of JavaScript, its implementation among other Ajax interfaces and various different web-based frameworks which allow you to create stunning and dynamic web pages. Raw JavaScript, as I said, isn't terribly popular, but you're going to encounter a lot of challenges when using this.

JavaScript is also commonly used with HTML5 and CSS3 to create browser-based games. These are becoming more popular as web pages are becoming increasingly capable of running complex animations. JavaScript offers a fantastic catalyst to all of these because it allows the formation of client-side scripts.

Don't misunderstand; knowing how JavaScript works is extremely useful. You can use this knowledge as a catalyst to other things. Once you're finished with this book, I'd recommend that you start looking into the various web frameworks that use JavaScript. There are numerous.

React.JS, Meteor.JS, Mithril.JS, and Vue.JS are all extremely popular because they allow you to easily build interactive and dynamic web pages. In the modern day, this is an extremely important utility and will greatly benefit you as a programmer.

You'll also find that Node.JS offers a solid server-side scripting implementation. It can stand against PHP as one of the more popular web-based server-side technologies, even though it's much younger than PHP. If you're interested in running your servers and queries efficiently and building generally broad web-based applications, then Node.JS is preferred.

Now, we're going to discuss how to program in raw JavaScript, which will prepare you for using any of these. Having a foundation in programming is incredibly important.

Chapter 3

How to Program in JavaScript

In this chapter, we're going to start diving into how one can program in JavaScript. There is a lot to cover in this chapter. So, we're going to start from the basics and work our way up as we cover all of the different topics and try to build a finite idea of what this language is capable of. By the end of this chapter, you're going to understand a plethora of different concepts related to programming. Strap in tight because this is where the bulk of the book is going to come in.

Setting Up

Setting up JavaScript is incredibly easy. If you have a web browser, then you have JavaScript. It's as simple as that. Web browsers have built-in implementation engines for JavaScript, as does any other programs that purport to run JavaScript, such as the game engines that we mentioned.

This means that running JavaScript doesn't entail you to do much. However, there is one thing that we need to take note of before we continue. While normally you can save JavaScript files on their own and work on them in that way, you can't debug them in a browser like this. In order to use your JavaScript in your browser and have your scripts run, you need to call those scripts in one way or another. In order to simplify this, we're going to create an HTML document using the script tags. Write the following code in a new file called first.htm:

```html
<html>
<head>
   <script>
            document.write("Hello world!\n");
   </script>
</head>
<body>
</body>
</html>
```

Go ahead and save this file and then open it in the web browser of your choice. You'll see the following:

```
Hello world!
```

With this, bravo! You've written your first JavaScript script. So, you may be wondering, what is the essential difference between putting data within your file's head tags and your file's body tags?

The head tag is usually reserved for any programmatic logic in HTML. You can put the script in your body tag, and it will work equally well. However, most of the time, the JavaScript would be saved to a *different* file and then from there be loaded into the web page rather than all of it being confined in the same HTML document. This is the simplest way of emulating this sort of functionality within the confines that we've currently developed.

Data and Variables

At this point, we will talk about a concept that's a little bit heftier: the concept of *data*, *value*, and *variables*. You're going to see these all the time in programming. So, it's important that we start to talk about it a little bit. Depending on how and why you're going to use JavaScript, this may not come up so much. It will still come up, for example, if you're going to focus primarily on modern web development but often in a more abstracted way. However, nonetheless, it's important that we cover this concept because it's foundational to pretty much in all programming, in addition to the fact that this concept is instrumental in understanding some of the later concepts that we're going to be covering. For this reason, we're going to go ahead and just assume that we need to learn it and do that.

So, let's start with a simpler quest before anything else: what is a value? In order to understand the other concepts here, you need to understand how computers process data. As we said in the very first chapter, computers don't understand things like humans do. Ultimately, they process things in a series of mathematical equations, after things have been abstracted into things that resemble nothing like the value which we gave. For example, the bitwise representation of any given number won't really resemble the number that was passed in. Likewise, when you're trying to work with characters and text on-screen, computers have no innate bearing on what any of this is or how it can be used; they don't have the innate capacity for language that we do. All they understand is calculations. So, they need a method by which they can take these abstract human concepts and convert them into smaller numbers that *they* can work with.

However, that doesn't really answer or question. It only gives an entry point. The point that I'm trying to make is that in the end, computers understand all different representations of ideas in different ways, whether those ideas are numbers, letters, or any other thing that you can form some kind of abstract idea out of.

All of these abstract ideas form the nucleus of an idea that is a little bigger – the idea of the *value*. A value is any given abstract representation of some idea. That value could be a number, a character, a set of characters, or none of the above. A value is the communication of an abstract idea that can *be* communicated.

Computers understand these values according to the *type* of value they are. Computers need different types because, again, all of the values that a computer can understand need to be converted from our abstract idea of these values into something that the computer can work with, that is, ones and zeroes. These separate kinds of data can be referred to succinctly as *data types*.

There are numerous different data types in JavaScript, and there even exists the ability to create your own. However, data types are a little bit like atoms; there comes a point where if you break a molecule down that is composed of different atoms, then eventually you just get singular atoms and can't go any further without getting to the subatomic level and dealing with things like particles and quarks and so forth.

Data types in JavaScript and programming, in general, are a bit the same. Every programming language has these nucleic data types that form the basis for all other kinds of data in the programming language. These types that can't be broken down any further are called *primitive* types, and every language has their own primitive types.

JavaScript specifically has six different primitive types, each with their own use cases and definitions. Here, we're going to talk about what these different primitive types are so that you will know what these primitive types can *do* and what different kinds of data you can store and manipulate in JavaScript.

string – String denotes a data type which is necessarily composed of just characters. Character here refers to anything that is alphanumeric or symbolic. Basically, character is any text which may be represented on a screen in a computer. String refers explicitly to the idea of these characters and not necessarily to the characters themselves. For example, if you have a string value that hold numbers, then you cannot add a given number to it, because the string numeric value will not be understood by the system as numbers themselves but just as a set of characters which represent numbers. This idea will make a bit more sense later on when we start discussing the idea of arrays.

number – Number denotes a data type that uses *any* number, whether those are whole, decimal, or any other kind of number. This slightly separates JavaScript from other programming languages. We'll talk about this more in-depth a little bit later on, but it's a pretty easy concept to grasp, so don't stress about it too much.

undefined – Undefined is the data type which belongs to any variable (which we'll discuss in a second) that doesn't have a value set to it just yet. *undefined* can also be returned in a given function, but we'll talk about that later as well when we start talking about functions in general.

null – Null in computer science refers to any number which doesn't *have* a value. Null is different from undefined because undefined values simply generally haven't had a value ascribed to them yet, whereas null finitely doesn't have a value affixed.

boolean – Booleans are another concept that will make more sense later on but for right now just understand booleans as pertaining to the idea of true or false. Booleans are thereby a little bit of a rougher concept to really completely understand, even if they appear incredibly simple.

symbol – Symbols are the hardest primitive to understand for a beginner, and, frankly, as a beginner, you aren't really going to need to know about them. So you can just forget about them for the time being. However, for necessity's sake, we needed to cover it.

All of these also have *object* wrappers, which are another concept we'll talk about later in the chapter. I know, I know, it seems like I'm introducing a whole lot of ideas without talking about them at all, but don't worry. I promise we'll get to *all* of this in due time.

So why is this information important? What can one do with this knowledge? Well, you can do a whole lot. For example, let's change the code that we had so that the document.write line reads like the following:

   document.write(4 + 3);

Save your file and refresh the page. You should be seeing the following:

```
7
```

See how intuitive that is? You can manipulate these pieces of data. We'll get to that in just a second after we talk about *variables*. Now that you know how data works, you're somewhat prepared to start working with this next concept. See, sometimes, obviously, you're going to want to keep data for more than just one instance as we did above. In these cases, you need a way to keep track of data.

This functionality is offered to you through *variables*. You can keep track of data using variables and then change the data later by referring to it by some name that you define. You can define variables in JavaScript as the following:

   var *variableName*;

You can also define it with an initial value. This is called initialization:

   var myBananas = 3;

Alternatively, you can declare a variable and then define its value later:

   var myBananas;
   myBananas = 3;

So, why does all of this go together? First, the reason why we need to talk about data types was that JavaScript doesn't make you keep up with what kind of data a variable holds. This is good in some ways because it honestly makes it a much easier language to learn that it might be otherwise compared to something like C++ where you have to explicitly declare what type of data you're working with. Meanwhile, this can be difficult for a beginner who doesn't exactly understand how data works and how computers understand data. So, let's just assume that you're still starting to learn JavaScript. I decided that it's best to discuss how all of this works as opposed to just throwing you into the fire and expecting you to figure it out on your own. I may have just saved you a bit of time and future troubleshooting!

You can print out variables the same way you can print out individual data. This is because variables essentially just serve as boxes which can hold values. You can reach into these boxes and change the values, but the box will retain the same number of variable and refer to whatever is placed within it. When you create a variable, you're creating a box which may hold values. When you refer to that variable, you're saying "hey, whatever is in the box with that name, I want to work with that."

Let's try this with the last piece of data. Change your script as follows:

```
var number1 = 4;
var number2 = 4;
var number3 = number1 + number2;
document.write(number3);
```

Save it and reload the page; you'll end up with the following:

8

If that's the case, then perfect! You're well on your way to being adept at JavaScript. This is only the beginning, but much more can be done from here.

You can create a string variable by assigning a value with quotes around it; quotes indicate that a value is a string value. Note, too, that when you create these variables in JavaScript, they aren't created as the primitives but rather as the object wrappers – which, again, we'll talk about more in-depth later. When you try to connect strings, you do what's called a *concatenation*, which is where the characters from both of the strings are put together into one bigger string.

Anyhow, it's time that we move on to the next major part of this chapter, which uses all the knowledge we gained so far. We need to start discussing *math*.

Math in JavaScript

Math in JavaScript isn't a terrible complicated thing. For the most part, it uses symbols that you're likely already familiar with. There won't be a whole lot for you to learn here, but rather this section is about taking the parts that you're most likely probably already familiar with and then using those in order to build a better base.

Math operations in JavaScript are written and carried out through the use of mathematical operators. These often will be very similar to their counterparts in other languages and, indeed, in math in general.

The operators in JavaScript are as follows:

    a + b

This is the *addition* operator, as you've already seen. This will add two things together. It can also be used to concatenate strings or to connect them. If you add a number to a string, then the number will be added *to* the string; for example "hello " + 5 would equal "hello 5."

    a - b

This is the *subtraction* operator. The subtraction operator is used to subtract one value from another, as you might predict.

a * b

This is the *multiplication* operator. This is used to multiply one thing by another.

a / b

This is the *division* operator. This is used to divide one number by another.

a % b

This is the modulo operator. This is used to find the remainder of a certain equation. For example, 5 % 2 would return 1 since 5 / 2 would give a remainder of 1.

a**b

This is the exponentiation operator. The exponentiation operator will raise a "to the power" of b and return that number.

These are the basic mathematical operators of JavaScript. You can use these to easily perform complex mathematical operations in JavaScript. This may not seem like a big deal right now, but as we press on through the chapter, you'll see why math, more or less, is essential in anything you may do with JavaScript (or programming in general).

The other important operators to cover are the assignment operators. You can use the assignment operators in order to change a value in shorthand.

Assignment operators take a variable and then use any of the above operators with an equals sign. This will assign a new value to that variable. The most obvious assignment operator is the *equals sign*, which is used to assign a value to the left variable of the right side of the expression.

a += b

This is equal to a = a + b.

a -= b

This is equal to a = a - b.

a *= b

This is equal to a = a * b.

a /= b

This is equal to a = a / b.

a %= b

This is equal to a = a % b.

There are two more shorthand operators, the increment and decrement operators. These can be used to add or subtract one from a given variable, *a++* and *a--*, respectively, where *a* is the name of the variable that you're trying to increment or decrement.

We've covered most of the basic arithmetic and assignment operators that you're going to need for JavaScript. Now we're going to use this knowledge to build a foundation for understanding programmatic logic, which is a great and important foundation for being able to use all these.

Foundations of Logic

So, why do we need to focus on logic specifically? What do we have to gain from it? The simple answer is that understanding logic allows you to let your computer understand logic. All of logic may be expressed in a mathematical way, and your computer, too, may come to understand logic in that sense. Computers, after all, are excellent at solving equations and able to make comparisons as a result of those equations.

This may not seem like a huge deal, but computers being able to think is a really good thing. Think about it; any time that your program is able to decide technically, it's using logic. You may not even have to think that hard. There are a lot of basic instances of logic. This will make more sense later on.

So what exactly is logic? Logic is, in one way or another, just a manner of systematically using statements. These statements can then be used to derive conclusions. Logic is used, often, in order to determine whether a given statement is true or false, both in computing and in real life.

Perhaps the most classic example of logic is in the old Socratic form: "All men are mortal; Socrates is a man; therefore, Socrates is mortal." This sort of transitive logic provides the foundation for much of what we know about *modern* logic and is perhaps one of the best examples of simple applications of logic used in different contexts.

Logic in computers is usually based on *expressions*. Expressions might be familiar to you from your old high school or college algebra courses, where you write out a certain statement written and determine if it's true or false. You can use algebra on these expressions to simplify them just by treating the expression operator as an equals sign.

This basic format stays the same. Expressions are essentially a method by which you can compare one value to another. You can set the standard of the comparison, for example, whether you're determining if two values are equivalent or not, if one is more or less than the other, so on. Expressions, therefore, are a great tool used in logic and play a part likewise in computer-based logic.

You form expressions through the use of logical operators. These logical operators are the very basis of expressions. The following are the logical operators that you can use in JavaScript:

$a == b$

This will compare value *a* to value *b* and return whether or not the two are equal to each other. If so, it will return true and false if otherwise.

    a === b

This will compare the two values and return true if they are both equal to each other *and* if they are of the same type.

    a != b

This will compare the two values and return true if they are *not* equal to each other *or* if they are not of the same type. This is logical *or*. So, they can be both *unequal* and *of the same type,* and it will still return true. I'll explain that later.

    a > b

This will determine if a is greater than b.

    a < b

This will determine if a is less than b.

    a >= b

This will determine if a is greater than or equal to b.

    a <= b

This will determine if a is less than or equal to b.

You can use these to form *individual expressions*. You can then use these expressions in logical statements, which will be discussed later. Note how these expressions return either true or false depending on whether they're true or not. This goes back to the boolean values that we discussed earlier. These return a boolean value, which may be either true or false depending on the statement.

Let's return to variables for a second. You can store a boolean value to a variable, like the following:

val myBool = true;

However, you can also store an *expression* to a variable, and it will store the true or false boolean value.

val myBool = 3 > 5;

The above would be false because 3 is obviously *not* greater than 5. Remember that the function of expressions is to compare values; therefore, you can compare any values. You can likewise compare variables instead of raw values. Make sure your variables are of the same type. If not, you might see some weird results in your comparison!

Anyway, you can chain these expressions into a longer expression to build more sophisticated logical systems. These systems will check *every* part of the greater expression to verify whether or not the logic behind them is true or not.

There are three more logical operators that we haven't covered yet which are tailored specifically toward the purpose of allowing you to build these larger expressions.

        expressionA && expressionB

This is the logical *and* operator which checks if both expressions A and B are true. If so, the entire expression will return true and false if otherwise.

        expressionA || expressionB

This is the logical *or* operator which checks if *either* expression A *or* B is true. If neither is true, then the entire expression will return false. If either expression is true, then the entire expression will return true. If, technically, one expression is true and the whole expression is true, then both expressions may be true since the technical limitation shows that either side is true and that it is satisfied even if both sides are true.

!(expression)

This is the logical, *not* operator. You can use this to test whether something is *not* true. If it's *not* true, then the entire expression will return true. If it *is* true, then the entire expression will return false.

Note that when you use these, you have to use the exact version that I've specified. For example, getting two equals signs but using one instead will significantly change the meaning of your expression. Likewise, using only one ampersand (&) or one pipe (|) sign will change the meaning of your expression at its very root by transforming it into a bitwise expression, that is, it will be evaluating things at the bit level or the smallest possible mathematical level that you're allowed access to by your computer. You cannot obtain the results that you wanted, *unless* you're specifically trying to do bitwise operations which, at this point, you almost certainly cannot. Just be cautious when working with these expressions.

With that said, hopefully, we've built a solid foundation of logical understanding. This is important because it's going to play a great role in the following sections of the chapter where we discuss the actual meat of control flow and all of the topics that make it up.

Control Flow 101: Conditional Statements

That foray into control flow starts right as we speak. We're going to discuss how you can use the expressions that we covered in the last part of this chapter to build conditional statements. Conditional statements are the first essential part of control flow.

You may be wondering what control flow is. Control flow is the method by which you can direct your computer to obtain rudimentary forms of logic. By using the control flow, you can direct your computer (for instance, your web page) to make different decisions based on the current state of the given data.

Conditional statements exist in two forms, active and passive conditionals. Passive conditionals are the most basic form. So, we're going to be covering those first.

Passive conditionals are based on the idea of evaluating a single expression and then taking action if it's true. If it's true, then the code within will be run. If the condition is evaluated and turns out to not be true, then the code will be skipped over.

The basic form of a passive conditional in control flow is as follows:

```
if (expression) {
    // code within
}
```

Expression is any expression constructed as we discussed earlier. This is called a passive conditional because it allows you to create a statement that doesn't *require* anything on the end of the interpreter. For example, it doesn't require that your interpreter run a code if it comes out that the condition is false. This means that the condition, if necessary, can be skipped over altogether.

However, sometimes you're going to want something else of your statement. For example, if the code runs and it turns out that the statement isn't true, then you can have a backup code that will run in lieu of the conditional code. This ensures that no matter what, an action is always taken, which also gives you an opportunity to create a "backup" clause for your conditional statement by implementing another condition.

The syntax for the active conditional is as follows:

```
if (expression) {
    // code goes here
} else {
    // code
}
```

165

This will evaluate the expression. If the expression turns out not true, then it will proceed to the else statement, run the code within it, and then proceed to the next part of the program, instead of entirely skipping over the conditional statement as a whole.

However, sometimes you may want to have yet another condition that you can evaluate. This is pretty easy to set up. You can do so through the implementation of *else if* statements. *Else if* statements allow you to easily establish secondary expressions to evaluate. In *else if* statements, the first given expression will be evaluated. If it turns out not true, then the second expression will be evaluated. You can set up as many *else if* statements as you want, but take note that after a certain point, it will stop setting them up over and over.

You can set up an *else if* statement as follows:

```
if (expression) {
    // code goes here
} else if (expression) {
    // code goes here
} else {
    // code goes here
}
```

That is how you set up active conditionals in order to ensure that some codes will always run in a conditional statement. However, take note that this is not always what you wanted to happen. There are many cases, for example, where you may just want to evaluate to see if a single condition has taken place and then retain that code if that's not the case. In these cases, it is better to use a passive conditional.

Arrays

Before we jump into the next part of the control flow, let us first discuss another extremely important concept: arrays. Arrays are a foundational part of programming, and they will inevitably find their way into your JavaScript programming. So, it's important that you understand arrays and how they function for you to be able to write better codes over the long term.

What exactly is an array? An array is a method of storing connected data together in an essential way. The use of an array may not be immediately obvious. Let us first take a look at arrays by imagining a scenario in which they *don't* exist. For example, let's say that we wanted to store all of the different guitar models that we had so that we can easily locate them later.

We could store the names of the guitars like the following:

val guitar1Name = "Gibson Les Paul";
val guitar2Name = "Fender Stratocaster";
val guitar3Name = "Ibanez s420WK";

As you can see above, this becomes very unwieldy very fast. It can be hard to access the data that you need. Additionally, if you are trying to increment through the data, for one reason or another, like listing all of the guitars that you own, you will have to do so in a sequential manner and slowly work through each variable, printing them out one by one.

This is not the best way to do this. The best way is to do it using an array. Arrays are implemented in many different ways across different programming languages, but the specific implementation of arrays in JavaScript is pretty simple, fortunately. Therefore, you will not encounter many issues in getting them to work, especially as opposed to a language like Java or C++ where they have far more rigid definitions to them which can be more complicated to set up.

Arrays are essentially a set of data, especially in the JavaScript implementation. Arrays allow you to store all of these in a single place and then refer to them by accessing them from that common location. In the original implementation of arrays, you can set up a memory in a contiguous manner such that it will be easy for the computer to refer to these locations and individual value storage locations. All of the data would literally be side by side, which allows you to easily work through this data piece by piece and access what you need instead of messing around with various different variable names and other confusing factors that might further complicate the development.

When you set up an array, you essentially set up individual side-by-side boxes of data, much like the variables that we discussed before. You can then access these boxes by referring to the location of the box. Imagine a bank's safety deposit room. There are several different boxes that you can reach for you to obtain a certain value, and you know which box to reach into by referring to its index.

How can we emulate this in our own code? What can we do there? We can set up our own safety deposit room, as a manner of speaking, and then refer to the box we want to reach into.

In order to do this, you must first declare an array (like any other value) and then feed it a set of data.

var guitars = ["Gibson Les Paul", "Fender Stratocaster", "Ibanez S420WK"];

See how simple that is? Now you can reach into this code and obtain your data any time you want. Let's test this out by creating this file for ourselves. Erase your current JavaScript and type the following:

var books = ["Moby Dick", "Pride and Prejudice", "Ulysses"];

Now, let's say that we want to print the first book from this set. How can we do that? First, we need refer to its safety deposit box. An individual piece of data from an array can be referred to as an *element*. Arrays are composed of many different elements which make up the entire array. These elements are located in different positions in the array, which are referred to as their *indices*, or an individual as an *index*. Array indices start at 0 due to practical computer science reasons that we aren't going to dig into right now.

So, if we want to print the first piece of data in this array, we can do that like the following:

```
var books = ["Moby Dick", "Pride and Prejudice", "Ulysses"];
document.write(books[0]);
```

If you save this and try to refresh your document, you will see the following:

Moby Dick

Easy, right? Know you can locate all the elements in the array. You can also reassign the value of a certain element by referring to its index and assigning it a new value, or you can use this as a means of printing or manipulating the data at these places. Now, let's say that we want to add an element to the array. How do we do it?

The easiest way is to use the *push* method. You simply call the push method and send it the argument of what data you want to add to your array. Let's test this out ourselves. Write the following code:

```
books.push("On the Road");
document.write("<br/>" + books[3]);
```

Save your page and then refresh it. You should see the following:

Moby Dick
On the Road

With that, we've worked through the basics of arrays. You're going to see why this is particularly useful in the next part of this chapter.

Control Flow 102: Loops

What exactly are loops and how can you use them? Loops are an integral part of logic and control flow. You may not realize it, but you use loop logic all the time.

Imagine this: you're sitting there trying to type a text message for your best friend or significant other or somebody. What do you do? It's really simple; you just type each character and then press send, right? But this is an application of loop logic in and of itself.

Think about it. First, you want to type a message, so you open your messaging app. Then, you start typing the message. You seek the character on your keyboard and then you press it and you verify that you pressed the right character. You do this for every character. You also check to see if you typed the final character of the message. Then, you press send and close the messaging app and the loop has been terminated. This is how you can think of many simple activities in terms of loop logic. We tend to not think about this too much because, let's be honest, it's not that fun of a topic to mull over. Regardless of that, it's an extremely important part of loop logic. Therefore, we're going to talk about it nonetheless.

In JavaScript, there are two main kinds of loops, *for loops* and *while loops*. These loops are both similar in terms of their essential logic (do something under these terms), but they have immensely different cases which entails us to use either of them. We're going to spend a bit of time examining these two loops and their optimal use cases in the next section.

Let's start with the easier one – the *while* loop. The while loop is pretty simple because, in a lot of ways, it just mirrors many of the topics that we've already discussed throughout the course of the chapter, specifically the *if* statement. The *while* loop works by repeatedly running through the code contained within it. On every iteration of the while loop, the loop will evaluate the stated condition and determine whether or not it is still true. If it does happen to be true, the loop will run again. The loop will continue to ad nauseum until it determines that the condition for the loop is not true after all. At this point, the loop will terminate and the code will move on to the next point. Hopefully, this is an adequate explanation, but just in case it isn't, don't worry, we're going to be looking at the structure of these now.

So, the structure of a while loop looks like the following:

```
while (expression) {
    // code here
}
```

Let's say, for example, that we want to count from 1 to 10 using this. First, we must define our variable just as the following:

```
var i = 0;
```

Now, we need to set up our while loop. This is going to run for as long as it is less than 10:

```
while (i < 10) {
}
```

On every iteration of this loop, we want to have an *i* increment by one (we'll use a pre-fix so that it prints *i* after it's been incremented rather than a post-fix), and we want to print that increment as well as an HTML line break. The code will end up looking like the following:

```
var i = 0;

while (i < 10) {
    document.write(++i + "<br />");
}
```

The outcome of this code will look like the following:

```
1
2
3
4
5
6
7
8
9
10
```

However, as you can see above, this isn't exactly the best way to do this. It's a little unwieldy and hard to understand, and you have to go out of your way to do some things that ideally you really wouldn't have to, such as defining a variable that you will use for the loop before you do so.

Loops are useful in checking singular conditions that will become false upon an event. In other words, loops are more preferred if you don't know *how long* a loop is going to run. For a loop like this, where you know exactly how many times it's going to run, it's better to use an incremental loop such as a *for* loop. We'll get to that momentarily.

Based on this, loops are commonly used in the form of a *game loop*. Game loops aren't only for games, of course. Game loops are called so because they follow the basic idea that games do.

A game loop has a certain boolean variable that is evaluated with every run of the loop. For example, you may have a boolean called *running* which is set to be true.

In games, you have a certain win or loss condition that must be met. Until this is met, the same thing will happen repeatedly. For instance, if a player hasn't fallen in lava or been hit three times, then that player is still alive! You don't know how long they'll stay alive, and therefore you don't know how many times you'll need to run your basic logical loop. So, you can't use an incremental loop. It is better to use the *while* loop instead for cases like this.

If you step in lava or your hit counter does hit 3, then you can set the variable running to false. This will indicate to the *while* loop that playtime is over, that the player has lost. Them you can quit running this internal logic and then proceed to the next part of the code, which is a game over screen presumably.

This is a vast simplification but hopefully it does a good job in explaining *what* a game loop is and why *while* loops are so well fit for them. *While* loops are very useful in terms of constantly evaluating a function and repeatedly running the logic in situations where the actual context surrounding it all vary tremendously. If you don't know exactly how much you're going to need to run the code, then *while* loops allow you to check that code for you to be able to obtain a more dynamic interpretation.

While loops are the opposite of *for loops*. *For* loops are used to *iterate* through the code. Instead of just repeatedly running the same chunk until a given condition isn't true, you can define the running terms of the function. This may not immediately make sense, but it will, don't worry.

Earlier, we talked about arrays and mentioned that one of the problems you may run into would be iterating through the guitar variables if you need to. The explanation of the arrays themselves didn't make much sense either in that context. Now, let's dive more into that.

Erase your code for the *while* loop and then bring back the book list code. It should look like the following:

```
books = ["Moby Dick", "Pride and Prejudice", "Ulysses"];
document.write(books[0]);
books.push("On the Road");
document.write("<br/>" + books[3]);
```

Now, let's say that we want to iterate through all these. Remove our write lines so that what remains is our declaration and push method. Then, create a *for* loop. How do for loops work?

For loops work on the basis of iterating through data, as we mentioned earlier. *For* loops have three parts. The first part is the initialization of an iterator variable. This iterator variable serves as the starting point of your loop's "counting". The second part is the condition. This is the condition under which your loop continues to run. This will often be similar to what it would be in a *while* loop of the same function, but sometimes there will be a small change made between them. The third part is the incrementation step. This is the step by which your initialized loop variable moves with every loop of the equation. If, for example, you were to set this to an increment by one (variable++), then on every run of the loop, this variable will change by a degree of one.

The structure of a *for* loop looks like the following:

```
for (initializer variable; condition of running; increment) {
    // code within
}
```

If we want to print every book on our list, what do we do first? Remember that array indices are accessed through referring to their element. These elements start at zero. By starting our initialization variable at 0 and then referring to the index by the initialization variable, we can move through our whole list of books!

Now, how do we define the running length of our loop? In order to define the running length of this loop, you must obtain the length of the array by accessing the array's *length* property.

Then, you must increment by 1 each time.

With all of that in mind, our loop will probably start to look like the following:

```
for (var i = 0; i < books.length; i++) {
```

```
        document.write(books[i] + "<br/>");
}
```

Our end code will also look like the following:

```
var books = ["Moby Dick", "Pride and Prejudice", "Ulysses"];
books.push("On the Road");
for (var i=0; i<books.length;i++) {
    document.write(books[i] + "br/>");
}
```

Now, save and run this code and see how it comes out. It should look a little bit like the following:

```
Moby Dick
Pride and Prejudice
Ulysses
On the Road
```

With that, perfect! You've made a working for loop in JavaScript. Now, let's talk about functions. Functions are an important catalyst for developing a great working knowledge of JavaScript.

Functions

What exactly *is* a function? A function, to some, may send a person back to memories of their old high school or college math courses where worked with things such as *f(x)* = *y*. In this function, the function *f()* takes an argument of *x*. The argument *x* can be manipulated by the function *f(x)* to produce the output of *y*.

However, there are, in fact, some differences between this definition of a function and the one that we're forced to work with in computer science. Computer science was, in many ways, developed as an extension of mathematics after all. It makes sense that computer science carries over many concepts from mathematics.

How do computer science functions differ? Computer science functions don't just have to take one argument. They also don't have to take *any* arguments. We'll talk about that in just a second. (There are some multivariable functions in higher-level mathematics, but this book isn't going to assume that you have that background.)

Computer science functions can take zero, one, or multiple arguments. These arguments can then be manipulated in the target data to give you a dynamic function to work with.

This is a parallel. For example, let *f(x) = 3x + 5 = y*. Let's say that we sent in the argument of *3* for this function. We substitute x for 3 since x is the argument and then obtain our final value *y*. 3(3) + 5 = 9 + 5 = 14 = y. Therefore, y = 14, and our function *returns* the value of 14.

Just as a function can *return* a value, our own functions can return values too. These functions can be the end result of all of the mathematics and operations that you did in the function. However, a function doesn't necessarily have to *return* anything either.

What is the purpose of functions then? Functions allow you to abstract certain chunks of code in your program that you're repeatedly reusing. This has many uses from a programmer's point of view, but perhaps the biggest deal is the fact that it makes your code more modular. It simplifies and makes things so that you can start using them in multiple different ways even if you use the same chunk of code, without the need for you to repeatedly reuse the code.

Let's work with this idea for a moment. Let's say that we need a function to return the volume of a given rectangular prism. The following is how you define a function in JavaScript:

```
function functionName(arguments) {
    // code
```

return value; // (if necessary)
}

Let's say that we want to develop a function that can return the volume of a prism. The volume of a prism is just length by width by height as follows:

```
function volumeOfPrism(length, width, height) {
    return length * width * height;
}
```

This will give back the value of the volume. This is one of the coolest parts of JavaScript and scripting in general. Just like any other values in JavaScript, you can save this to a variable and use it later. This gives you a lot of utility and flexibility as a programmer. You can also save it outside of a variable and just print the raw value of the function like the following:

```
document.write(volumeOfPrism(3,4,5));
```

This will print the value 60. You can save it like the following also:

```
volume = volumeOfPrism(3,4,5);
```

This will store the value of volume as 60, which you can then verify by printing it out:

```
document.write(volume);
```

Now, with all of that said, let's cover the last topic. We will not cover it entirely in-depth, but it's important that we do so that you will be aware of what you're dealing with.

Object-Oriented Programming: An Introduction

We're not going to tackle all the complex coding of object-oriented programming right now. We're just going to be dealing with the raw concepts at heart: classes and objects. In order to understand these, we must first discuss classes. This will make some of the things that we said earlier – like object wrappers – make more sense.

What is a class? The utility of classes comes from the fact that sometimes you need more complex structures than what the code automatically gives you. This occurs rarely in languages like JavaScript. Object-oriented programming is about this abstraction at its core: the ability to take smaller concepts and then integrate them into bigger structures that utilize these concepts.

A better way to think about it is to try to imagine a dog. All dogs have features in common; for example, they have 2 eyes, 4 legs, and a wagging tail. They can also bark. However, there can be a lot of variance, too. For example, dogs can have separate breeds and other things which set them apart, like their size or weight.

However, there are still unifying concepts and properties that apply to all dogs, regardless their breed, size, and weight, which are *properties* they all have in common. These can be portrayed as individual data members of a larger structure. This structure can be referred to as a *dog*. These individual data members are called the properties of the dog class. Each class can also have standard functions, like *bark* or *wagTail*, which are common among all instances of the class.

A singular instance of a class is referred to as an object. Each object has its own name and can be treated as its own variable. So, if you define a class *dog*, you can create a dog variable known as *myDog* or any other standard variable name. Then, access the properties and alter them however you wish. This standardization and abstraction are the major appeals of object-oriented programming.

Therefore, whenever something is referred to as an *object*, it means that a class was constructed which consists of smaller data types and pieces of data that all make up the bigger concept that is represented both through the object and through its constituent class.

With that, we've worked through the bulk of the stuff that you need to know as an new JavaScript programmer. These are the foundations of all the knowledge you gained from this book, and it's important that you understand all these before continuing.

Chapter 4

The Future of JavaScript

At this point, you might be wondering, what exactly is the future of JavaScript? What can I expect to gain from learning all these?

Since the whitepaper that brought Ajax to the forefront, JavaScript has only been gaining steam constantly. There are a huge number of new JavaScript frameworks that are being introduced every year that are fantastic for their various different purposes, and more frameworks will be expected.

The future of JavaScript is more about the future of you. JavaScript is only going to become more popular if further features are added into the future ECMA standardizations, if the web in general is used by more people, and if web platforms mature. Likewise, JavaScript matures alongside PHP and CSS. It is expected that JavaScript will continue to develop in the future.

If you want to be a web developer, you must learn JavaScript and be aware of its frameworks, because those will allow you to keep up with the trends.

As technology grows more and more advanced, JavaScript programmers will also be more in demand. There are a number of things right now that are currently relegated to other common scripting languages, like Python, that can be ported to JavaScript. Natural language processing and machine translation are just two examples that will inevitably be ported to JavaScript which therefore increases demand.

JavaScript isn't just for creating pretty web pages; the actual utility of web pages is expanding. With this in mind, JavaScript will advance to this because web pages are now able to perform very complicated actions. The advent of browser-based HTML/CSS/JavaScript games only goes to support this.

As a JavaScript programmer, expect that more programmers will be needed in the industry. Therefore, one of the best things that you can do for yourself is to learn JavaScript and advance your learning.

Conclusion

Thank you for making it through the end of *JavaScript*. Let's hope that it was informative and able to provide you with all of the tools you need to achieve your goals whatever they may be.

The next step is to use this knowledge. Get out there and start working with some JavaScript frameworks. The way to reinforce all that you've learned is by doing it. You won't be familiar with all of them, and sometimes you're even going to be left really confused, but if you keep pushing through, then I guarantee that it will be worth it and you'll come out the other end as a fantastic web developer.

Lastly, if you found this book useful in anyway, a review on Amazon is always appreciated!

Made in the USA
Coppell, TX
04 October 2022